SOCIETY AND KNOWLEDGE

WORLD PERSPECTIVES

Volumes already published

WORLD PERSPECTIVES · *Volume Six*

Planned and Edited by RUTH NANDA ANSHEN

SOCIETY AND KNOWLEDGE

By V. G. CHILDE, F.B.A., D. Litt., D.Sc.

Professor of Prehistoric European Archaeology and
Director of the Institute of Archaeology at the
University of London

GREENWOOD PRESS, PUBLISHERS
WESTPORT, CONNECTICUT

The Library of Congress has catalogued this publication as follows:

Library of Congress Cataloging in Publication Data

Childe, Vere Gordon, 1892-1957.
  Society and knowledge.

  Original ed. issued as v. 6 of World perspectives.
  1. Knowledge, Sociology of. I. Title.
[BD175.C54 1973]   121   72-10690
ISBN 0-8371-6620-9

Originally published in 1956
by Harper & Brothers, New York

Reprinted with the permission
of Harper & Row, Publishers, Inc.

First Greenwood Reprinting 1973

Library of Congress Catalogue Card Number 72-10690

ISBN 0-8371-6620-9

Printed in the United States of America

Contents

World Perspectives

WORLD PERSPECTIVES is dedicated to the concept of man born out of a universe perceived through a fresh vision of reality. Its aim is to present short books written by the most conscious and responsible minds of today. Each volume represents the thought and belief of each author and sets forth the interrelation of the changing religious, scientific, artistic, political, economic and social influences upon man's total experience.

This Series is committed to a re-examination of all those sides of human endeavor which the specialist was taught to believe he could safely leave aside. It interprets present and past events impinging on human life in our growing World Age and envisages what man may yet attain when summoned by an unbending inner necessity to the quest of what is most exalted in him. Its purpose is to offer new vistas in terms of world and human development while refusing to betray the intimate correlation between universality and individuality, dynamics and form, freedom and destiny. Each author treats his subject from the broad perspective of the world community, not from the Judaeo-Christian, Western, or Eastern viewpoint alone.

Certain fundamental questions which have received too little consideration in the face of the spiritual, moral and political world crises of our day, and in the light of technology which has released the creative energies of peoples, are treated in these books. Our authors deal with the increasing realization that spirit and nature are not separate and apart; that intuition and reason must regain their importance as the means of perceiving and fusing inner being with outer reality.

World Perspectives endeavors to show that the conception of organism is a higher and more concrete conception than that of matter and energy. Thus it would seem that science itself must ultimately pursue the aim of interpreting the physical world of matter and energy in terms of the biological conception of organism. An enlarged meaning of life, of biology, not as it is revealed in the test tube of the laboratory but as it is experienced within the organism of life itself is attempted in this Series. For the principle of life consists in the tension which connects spirit with the realm of matter. The element of life is dominant in the very texture of nature, thus rendering life, biology, a trans-empirical science. The laws of life have their origin beyond their mere physical manifestations and compel us to consider their spiritual source. In fact, the widening of the conceptual framework has not only served to restore order within the respective branches of knowledge, but has also disclosed analogies in man's position regarding the analysis and synthesis of experience in apparently separated domains of knowledge suggesting the possibility of an ever more embracing objective description.

Knowledge, it is shown, no longer consists in a manipulation of man and nature as opposite forces, nor in the reduction of data to mere statistical order, but is a means of liberating mankind from the destructive power of fear, pointing the way toward the goal of the rehabilitation of the human will and the rebirth of faith and confidence in the human person. The works published also endeavor to reveal that the cry for patterns, systems and authorities is growing less insistent as the desire grows stronger in both East and West for the recovery of a dignity, integrity and self-realization which are the inalienable rights of man who may now guide change by means of conscious purpose in the light of rational experience.

Other vital questions explored relate to problems of international understanding as well as to problems dealing with prejudice and the resultant tensions and antagonisms. The growing perception and responsibility of our World Age point to the new reality that the individual person and the collective person supplement and integrate each other; that the thrall of totalitarianism of both right and left has been shaken in the universal desire to recapture the authority of truth and human totality. Mankind can finally place its trust not in a proletarian authoritarianism, not in a secularized humanism, both of which have betrayed the spiritual property right of history, but in a sacramental brotherhood and in the unity of knowledge, a widening of human horizons beyond every parochialism, and a revolution in human thought comparable to the basic assumption, among the ancient Greeks, of the sovereignty of reason; corresponding to the great effulgence of the moral conscience articulated by the Hebrew prophets; analogous to the fundamental assertions of Christianity; or to the beginning of a new scientific era, the era of the science of dynamics, the experimental foundations of which were laid by Galileo in the Renaissance.

An important effort of this Series is to re-examine the contradictory meanings and applications which are given today to such terms as democracy, freedom, justice, love, peace, brotherhood and God. The purpose of such inquiries is to clear the way for the foundation of a genuine *world* history not in terms of nation or race or culture but in terms of man in relation to God, to himself, his fellow man and the universe, that reach beyond immediate self-interest. For the meaning of the World Age consists in respecting man's hopes and dreams which lead to a deeper understanding of the basic values of all peoples.

Today in the East and in the West men are discovering that they are bound together, beyond any divisiveness, by a more fundamental unity than any mere agreement in thought and doctrine. They are beginning to know that all men possess the same primordial desires and tendencies; that the domination of man over man can no longer be justified by any appeal to God or nature; and such consciousness is the fruit of the spiritual and moral revolution through which humanity is now passing.

World Perspectives is planned to gain insight into the meaning of man, who not only is determined by history but who also determines history. History is to be understood as concerned not only with the life of man on this planet but as including also such cosmic influences as interpenetrate our human world.

This generation is discovering that history does not conform to the social optimism of modern civilization and that the organization of human communities and the establishment of justice, freedom and peace are not only intellectual achievements but spiritual and moral achievements as well, demanding a cherishing of the wholeness of human personality and constituting a never-ending challenge to man, emerging from the abyss of meaninglessness and suffering, to be renewed and replenished in the totality of his life. "For as one's thinking is, such one becomes, and it is because of this that thinking should be purified and transformed, for were it centered upon truth as it is now upon things perceptible to the senses, who would not be liberated from his bondage." [1]

There is in mankind today a counterforce to the sterility and danger of a quantitative, anonymous mass culture, a new, if sometimes imperceptible, spiritual sense of convergence toward world unity on the basis of the sacredness of each human person and respect for the plurality of cultures. There is a growing awareness that equality and justice are not to be evaluated in mere numerical terms but that they are proportionate and analogical in their reality.

We stand at the brink of the age of the world in which human life presses forward to actualize new forms. The false separation of man and nature, of time and space, of freedom and security, is acknowledged and we are faced with a new vision of man in his organic unity and of history offering a richness and diversity of quality and majesty of scope hitherto unprecedented. In relating the accumulated wisdom of man's spirit to the new reality of the World Age, in articulating its thought and belief, *World Perspectives* seeks to encourage a renaissance of hope in society and of pride in man's decision as to what his destiny will be.

The experience of dread, in the pit of which contemporary man has been plunged through his failure to transcend his existential limits, is the experience of the problem of whether he shall attain to being through the knowledge of himself or shall not, whether he shall annihilate nothingness or whether nothingness shall annihilate him. For he has been forced back to his origins as a result of the atrophy of the meaning of existence, and his anabasis may begin once more through his mysterious greatness to re-create his life.

The suffering and hope of this century have their origin in

[1] Maitri Upanishad, 6, 34, 4, 6.

the interior drama in which the spirit is driven as a result of
the split within itself, and in the invisible forces which are
born in the heart and mind of man. This suffering and this
hope arise also from material problems, economic, political,
technological. History itself is not a mere mechanical unfolding of events in the center of which man finds himself as a
stranger in a foreign land. The specific modern emphasis on
history as progressive, the specific prophetic emphasis on God
as acting only through history, and the specific Christian emphasis on the historical nature of revelation must now sur-
render to the new history embracing the new cosmology—a
profound event which is in the process of birth in the womb
of that invisible universe which is the mind of man.

This is the crisis in consciousness made articulate through
the crisis in science. This is the new awakening after a long
history which had its genesis in Descartes' denial that
theology could exist as a science, on the one hand, and on
the other, in Kant's denial that metaphysics could exist as a
science. Some fossilized forms of such positivistic thinking
still remain. However, it is now conceded, out of the influences of Whitehead, Bergson, and some phenomenologists,
that in addition to natural science with its tendency to isolate
quantitative values there exists another category of knowledge wherein philosophy, utilizing its own instruments, is
able to grasp the essence and innermost nature of the Absolute, of reality. The mysterious universe is now revealing to
philosophy and to science as well an enlarged meaning of
nature and of man which extends beyond mathematical and
experimental analysis of sensory phenomena. This meaning
rejects the mechanistic conception of the world and that positivistic attitude toward the world which considers philosophy
as a kind of mythology adequate only for the satisfaction of

emotional needs. In other words, the fundamental problems of philosophy, those problems which are central to life, are again confronting science and philosophy itself. Our problem is to discover a principle of differentiation and yet relationship lucid enough to justify and to purify both scientific and philosophical knowledge by accepting their mutual interdependence.

Justice itself, which has been "in a state of pilgrimage and crucifixion" and now is slowly being liberated from the grip of social and political demonologies in the East as well as in the West, begins to question its own premises. These modern revolutionary movements which have challenged the sacred institutions of society by protecting social injustice in the name of social justice are also being examined and reevaluated.

When we turn our gaze retrospectively to the early cosmic condition of man in the third millennium, we observe that the concept of justice as something to which man has an inalienable right began slowly to take form and, at the time of Hammurabi in the second millennium, justice, as inherently a part of man's nature and not as a beneficent gift to be bestowed, became part of the consciousness of society. This concept of human right consisted in the demand for justice in the universe, a demand which exists again in the twentieth century through a curious analogy. In accordance with the ancient view, man could himself become a god, could assume the identity of the great cosmic forces in the universe which surrounded him. He could influence this universe, not by supplication, but by action. And now again this consciousness of man's just relationship with the universe, with society and with his fellow men, can be actualized, and again not through supplication but through action.

Though never so powerful materially and technologically, Western democracy, with its concern for the sacredness of the human person gone astray, has never before been so seriously threatened morally and spiritually. National security and individual freedom are in ominous conflict. The possibility of a universal community and the technique of degradation exist side by side. There is no doubt that evil is accumulated among men in their passionate desire for unity. And yet, confronted with this evil, confronted with death, man, from the very depths of his soul, cries out for justice. Christianity in history could only reply to this protest against evil by the Annunciation of the Kingdom, by the promise of Eternal Life—which demanded faith. But the spiritual and moral suffering of man had exhausted his faith and his hope. He was left alone. His suffering remained unexplained.

However, man has now reached the last extremity of denigration. He yearns to consecrate himself. And so, among the spiritual and moral ruins of the West and of the East a renaissance is prepared beyond the limits of nihilism, darkness and despair. In the depths of the spiritual night, civilization with its many faces turning toward its source, may rekindle its light in an imminent second dawn—even as in the last book of Revelation, which speaks of a Second Coming with a New Heaven, a New Earth, and a new religious quality of life.

> And I saw a new heaven and a new
> earth; for the first heaven and the
> first earth were passed away.[2]

In spite of the infinite obligation of men and in spite of their finite power, in spite of the intransigence of national-

[2] Revelation 21:1.

isms, and in spite of spiritual bereavement and moral decay, beneath the apparent turmoil and upheaval of the present, and out of the transformations of this dynamic period with the unfolding of a world consciousness, the purpose of *World Perspectives* is to help quicken the "unshaken heart of well-rounded truth" and interpret the significant elements of the World Age now taking shape out of the core of that un-dimmed continuity of the creative process which restores man to mankind while deepening and enhancing his communion with the universe.

RUTH NANDA ANSHEN

New York, 1956

SOCIETY AND KNOWLEDGE

I.

The Prehistory of Knowledge

IN A book on philosophy the reader should be warned at the outset what the author is like. For this is going to be a book about philosophy—or rather that part of philosophy dignified with the imposing title "epistemology" or "theory of knowledge." Yet I am not a professional philosopher. I have indeed read a lot of philosophical classics, mostly in the original, works like Plato's *Republic,* Aristotle's *Politics,* Kant's *Kritik,* Hegel's *Phänomenologie des Geistes*—and plenty of more recent works from Marx to Wiener. But I do not intend to embroider this discourse with learned allusions or erudite quotations; I am frankly incapable of starting off with an historical survey from the Presocratics to the Logical Positivists. For I am by profession an archaeologist, and a prehistoric archaeologist at that.

As an archaeologist I deal with concrete, material things as much as any natural scientist. But as a pre*historian* I must treat my objects always and exclusively as concrete expressions and embodiments of human thoughts and ideas—in a word of knowledge. On the other hand as a *pre*historian I can never deal with individuals as a literary historian can; my objects must always be members of a class. Thus I could not recognize the first locomotive, still less its inventor, Stevenson. I could indeed recognize that Rocket I must be a very early specimen of the class of objects termed locomotives, but without written documents to help me I could not prove that it was really the earliest of all my locomotives. I could not classify it at all but for the fact that plenty of other locomotives have since been made and are being made today and that they all embody the same fundamental ideas as the Rocket, despite all improvements subsequently introduced. And what is true of railroad engines is true also of much earlier and seemingly simpler inventions like knives or axes. The first knife was undoubtedly made of stone, and, as a prehistorian, I can recognize many very old kinds of stone knives; I can subdivide the class into many subclasses or types. I may hope to be able to decide which type is the oldest. I can never spot the very oldest specimen of the type —the first knife ever made.

Now why can I recognize a class of objects termed "locomotives" and another of things called "knives"? If Rocket I had been unique, it would have slipped through my net of archaeological classification. But Robert Stevenson found a market for locomotives; he had apprentices and imitators. Just for these reasons Rocket I is the first member of a class of objects termed "locomotives." In rather more technical terms, Rocket I satisfied the demands of a society of persons interested in the transportation of goods and people and possessing capital to pay for locomotives and tracks. At the same time Stevenson founded a school of engineers and designers to whom he communicated his inventions and who were thereby enabled to reproduce and improve upon them. Still more briefly Stevenson's invention met a social need and was adopted and perpetuated by a corporation of engineers and technicians who had been initiated by the inventor. If no one had wanted locomotives or if Stevenson had not trained others to design and make them, the Rocket would be just a curio and not a subject for scientific archaeological study and classification. There is a class "locomotives" because, and only because, there has been and still is a society which uses locomotives and knows how to make them.

This is true of all archaeological classes as contrasted with the objects classified by the natural sciences. Of course the differences between types within a single archaeological class —for instance between English and American table knives or English and Russian locomotives today—are often mainly due to divergences in "fashion," to divergent social traditions of what constitutes good table manners or of what a railway engine should look like. Yet our types are indications and expressions of knowledge too as well as of use and fashion. A great deal of knowledge, indeed of science, went into the making of Rocket I and is embodied and crystallized in the product. And it was not only, nor even mainly, the private personal knowledge of Stevenson, the information he had accumulated from individual experience in his lifetime. He utilized, as well as enlarged, the public knowledge of English society in the early nineteenth century. He had learned what his forerunners—Newcomen, Watt, and the rest—had discovered about steam engines, valves, iron founding, thermodynamics. He utilized too the trained technical skill of a veritable army of anonymous mechanics and draughtsmen. Without their trained proficiency and dexterity, the Rocket would have remained a dream, like the siege engines of Leonardo da Vinci, or at best a toy, like the automata devised eighteen hundred years earlier by Hero of Alexandria.

So it would be unjust and arrogant to refuse the name "knowledge" to the technical skill—the "know-how"—of the intelligent artisan, just as it is impossible to deny the name of science to the applications of "pure" mathematics and "pure" physics that produced radar and nuclear weapons. In this latter sense any tool, however simple, even the stone knife of mammoth-hunters in the Ice Age, is an expression of knowledge—knowledge of the most suitable stone, of the properties of that stone, of how to strike it to produce a usable flake and of how to use the flake produced. But once more of public knowledge, for the knife is a type. Unless it were the first of its kind ever made, the maker did not have to find out for himself the proper shape, still less how and from what to make it. The society into which he was born through the words and example of his elders taught him what stone to select, how to make a knife from it and how to use it when made. All the requisite information was stored up in a social tradition of public knowledge.

Now I am writing not a treatise on archaeological interpretation, but a philosophical account of knowledge. As an archaeologist I have just introduced a slice from my annual course on archaeological method to explain my approach to what professional philosophers have made the problem of knowledge. I hope it will help the reader to realize the meaning I intend to give the word and why in my title "knowledge" is coupled with "society." To deserve the name, I contend, knowledge must be communicable and in that sense public and also useful, I mean, capable of being translated into successful action. The first qualification may come as a shock to mystics, whether religious or not. The second would certainly scandalize a Greek of the age of Plato and Aristotle and many academic scientists today who follow them in the pursuit of "science for its own sake." I am not in fact going to argue that these latter are suffering from a delusion, still less that they ought to be denied opportunities for doing "useless" research. An immense amount of very useful knowledge was acquired in precisely such disinterested research; in mathematics in particular this is constantly happening. It was about two thousand years before any practical use was found for Greek discoveries of the properties of harmonic series. At long last they proved fundamental for the development of probability theory as applied to insurance. Anyhow no one has yet found any practical use for archaeology. But I remain an archaeologist and claim the title of science for the information archaeology accumulates. At the same time, as a prehistorian, I am bound to make statements about the science or knowledge possessed even by preliterate peoples in the past though in this case all that archaeology can reveal is the practical applications made of such knowledge.

The archaeologists' claim to deduce preliterate science from its applications is in its turn an assertion of the practical character of knowledge. This assertion may be justified by an argument drawn from an allied branch of natural science—biology. Every living thing, every organism, lives by virtue of exchanges between it and its environment, between its body and what surrounds it. To live it must get "fuel"—food, water, oxygen, carbon dioxide—from outside itself. To enable the organism to do the needful, it must be provided with some rudimentary nerve apparatus to convey messages from outside its body. And generally the organism has to make some movement for the absorption of food, for avoidance of danger or for sexual reproduction. These movements take place in response to some change in the environment termed a "stimulus," of which the organism is made aware by a message through its nerve. In the simplest organisms the mechanism works quite automatically. The movement technically termed the response takes place whenever the receptor nerve is excited or, in scientific jargon, whenever the appropriate stimulus is presented. The clam shuts up, whenever any shadow interrupts the supply of light normally reaching its "optic nerve." This is what psychologists call "reflex action." The stimulus-response reflex is built into the creature's bodily structure. It is innate and transmitted biologically from parents to offspring just as much as the circulation of the blood (if any). The creature responds to the stimulus, the first time it is presented, just as well as on any later occasion.

You may if you like say that a clam "knows how" to close its shell or a stickleback "knows how" to respond to its mate's advances, but "knowledge" will not be used in that sense here. It would be rather more legitimate to say that an established reflex possessed by all members of a species represents the accumulated experience or knowledge common to the species as a whole. It is at least true that the species benefited by the experience of those who possessed the reflex, but only in this sense: they alone survived to reproduce; any who did not died off without offspring. But after all, could you not say as much of a single bodily organ? Yet no one would allege that a kidney represents the accumulated knowledge of any species, not even of Homo sapiens.

At a higher level in the evolutionary hierarchy, reflexes can be modified by experience; creatures can learn. The capacity of adapting responses in the light of results has been an immense advantage to the fortunate animals in the evolutionary race for survival as fittest. But it can be explained or described quite satisfactorily in terms of what Pavlov called "conditioned reflexes." And it can be simulated adequately in relatively simple electronic machines. The trouble is that

responses learned in this way by individual experience, individual trial and error, remain the private possession of the
learner.

For instance, rats learn to find their way out of a maze.
Once having found the clue by a long process of trial and
error, a rat will escape more quickly on each subsequent experiment till it soon learns to take the right turns at once. It
"knows the way out." But it cannot pass on this knowledge
to its progeny. Professor McDougall bred several generations
of trained rats, but his experiments failed to show any statistically significant improvement in the performance of the
latest generation. Still less can one rat teach another what
to do if it should be put in the middle of a maze. Its knowledge of the way out remains its private prerogative. As for
electronic machines, they have no progeny—at least I have
not heard of one that can reproduce its kind. Nor I think has
any engineer yet constructed a whole battery of electronic
machines that pool the information they have severally acquired. This could doubtless be done. But the activity of the
products would simulate not animal learning but a higher
level of knowing.

Man is the only animal that can communicate knowledge
acquired by experience to other members of the species. A
man, having found the way out of a maze by trial and error,
could not only himself remember how to proceed if he found
himself in the centre again; he could also tell his children and
anyone, quite unrelated to him by blood, how to proceed,
and that before they entered the maze at all. His knowledge,
though derived from personal experiences and personally
memorized, is communicable and, if communicated, public.
That is an observable peculiarity of human behavior and may
serve as an empirical criterion to distinguish human knowl-

edge from other kinds of knowledge or awareness. Strictly speaking the term knowledge should be confined to information that is thus communicable.

A man learns, not only, like a rat, from his private individual experiences, but also from the collective experience of a society, of all men, alive or dead, who have transmitted, or can transmit, to him the fruits of their experience—the ways they have found of escaping from mazes or of coping with other situations that do recur. It is this capacity of communicating the results of experience that has earned for our species its unique success in the biological competition for survival. Man, unprotected by fur or wool, by swiftness of foot or sharpness of tooth and claw, against the inclemencies of climate and the attacks of beasts of prey, has learned to make fire, clothes, houses, weapons, machines that enable him to live anywhere and vanquish the most powerful beasts of prey. That he has achieved not just because man is endowed with a capacity to make tools—i.e., not just because he can find out by trial and error how to fashion with his hands what he needs to supplement his bodily deficiencies—but rather because he can learn to make tools from others who have gone through some steps of the experimental process themselves.

If Stevenson had had to start from scratch where the "first man" started, he would never have designed a locomotive; his inventive genius might have found expression in a particularly stylish stone knife! The biological utility of communicable information is perhaps more obvious still in its negative application. Homo sapiens seems to be literally omnivorous. No innate appetite guides a weaned child what to eat as it impels a calf to eat grass. Many poisons look eminently appetizing. If men had to learn their avoidance by trial and error, human mortality would have been so heavy that the species would hardly have multiplied. Just as organisms with several reflex responses have managed better to survive and to multiply more economically than those more scantily equipped, just as animals that can learn by experience are still better fitted to survive and reproduce their kind, so men, who can learn from one another's experiences, have been the most successful species biologically. If then we say that historically the biological function of knowledge has been to ensure the survival and multiplication of Homo sapiens, we are not in fact importing into biology an extraneous teleological idea any more than when we say the same of the clam's shadow-closure reflex or the rat's capacity to learn by experience. Biologically all mechanisms for controlling and directing any organism's behavior in accordance with environmental conditions have proved their utility, and have themselves survived, by enabling their possessors to survive and multiply. Communicable knowledge is just the latest in time and the most successful of such mechanisms. Who can then deny that knowledge is useful at least biologically?

The foregoing peculiarity of human knowledge is bound up with, and correlative to, another human peculiarity—that which in turn makes archaeology possible. To the archaeologist man is the tool-making animal. Man makes tools because he has to. All other animals are born with specialized corporeal organs for acquiring food, preserving body temperature, escaping predators, and so on. They do not have to be taught how to make these or how to use them; their use is as innate as sucking is with human infants. Man is exceptionally ill equipped by nature in all these respects: His teeth are not adapted for cropping grass like a deer's, or for kill-ing deer like a tiger's; he has no fur nor even body hair to keep out cold. Neither exceptional fleetness enables man, like a gazelle, to escape carnivorous beasts nor do protective disguises allow him to elude them as a hare might. These deficiencies, as we have said, are more than counterbalanced by the "capacity" to make fire, tools and so on.

But this "capacity" is not an innate instinct. A caterpillar at the appropriate season proceeds to spin a most elaborate cocoon though it could never have seen any other caterpillar executing the feat. A human infant today, if left to itself and not given matches, displays no innate capacity for making fire, no aptitude for tearing up skins and sewing them together nor for selecting flint pebbles and turning them into knives. There is not the least reason to suppose that its first ancestors, several hundred thousand years ago, were any more richly endowed by nature. They too had to learn how to kindle fire, to make clothes and fashion knives. The very first men had to find out by trial and error. We are spared that sort of learning; it is from our elders we have learned how to control fire, how to use tools and perhaps how to make them. Our seniors transmit their knowledge to us. The same sort of transmission of knowledge has been going on for at least four hundred thousand years. So long ago archaeologists can recognize standardized tools—flint implements all conforming to a single model. Museums contain literally hundreds of thousands of so-called hand axes—pieces of stone all reduced to a geometrically similar form by the same process of chipping—that have been collected from all parts of Western Europe, Africa and Southwestern Asia. It is statistically impossible that individual stoneworkers all over the Old World should independently have hit upon just this odd shape and have reproduced it again and again for centuries by pure chance. Both the form of the hand axe and the technique for its manufacture must have been handed on by social tradition from generation to generation. Each standardized hand axe is thus the fossilized result of a bit of knowledge in a sense that a human nose or any other bodily organ emphatically is not.

From the seeming irrelevancies of this archaeological gossip some concrete meaning for the ambiguous term "knowledge" should yet have been emerging. It has at least been distinguished from instinctive "responses" and from what popular psychology terms "memories," as long as such remain personal and private. The knowledge embodied in the hand axes of the Old Stone Age was both useful and public. It enabled our remote precursors or ancestors to make serviceable tools such as they needed to supplement the deficiencies of their limbs and other bodily organs. And it was communicated to and transmitted by all the human beings who made hand axes for thousands of generations. Thus this knowledge was preserved—but not only preserved. It was also enriched and extended. During the two or three hundred thousand years over which hand axes were being made, archaeologists can detect improvements in their form and changes in the techniques of manufacture. More efficient tools were produced with less effort. These progressive changes reflect additions to knowledge, discoveries and inventions that were made public and incorporated in the traditional lore or knowledge used, transmitted and maintained by Old Stone Age societies. Of course the progressive change observed in archaeologists' "hand axes" is just one case of the general technological progress from simple manual tools of stone and bone to complicated machines made of metallic alloys and other artificial substances and operated by electrical or even nuclear power. It is this technological progress that has secured for Homo sapiens the victory over all competitors in the evolutionary race for survival. But technological progress in its turn is just the result and consequence of the accumulation of knowledge. That accumulation was possible just because human knowledge is public; one member of the species can communicate to another what he has found out.

Finally our unique evolutionary success is due not only to our ability to communicate knowledge, but equally to our capacity to use the symbols with which we communicate also for "reasoning." For reasoning has been defined as "operating with symbols in the head instead of going through a physical process of trial and error." Clearly Stevenson could never have invented the Rocket by messing about with full-scale pieces of cast iron and brass, filing bits down, casting bits on, sticking together and taking apart. He worked out the design in mathematical symbols, diagrams and perhaps scale models. To symbols and their role in reasoning and knowing we shall return again in Chapter IV. But first the distinction between knowing and remembering needs further elaboration. It is in fact important enough to deserve a chapter to itself.

II.

Knowing and Remembering

FOR understanding the distinction a concrete instance may be more helpful than several pages of abstract argumentation.

Suppose you and I are invited out to dinner at a friend's house in a London suburb. He begins to direct us: "Take the Piccadilly Line to Cranberry Park . . ." But here we interrupt him, each saying, "I know the way." I have in fact been there before. But I have forgotten the name of the street and the number of the house—and in any case street names and house numbers have become illegible since 1939. Yet when I emerge from the tube station, I at once recall the broad street with trolley buses on it and some sort of Protestant church almost opposite the station. I remember crossing that street and turning left, and so I do tonight. Then when I have gone some way, I notice a grocer's shop and pillar-box and a street corner. I am sure I used to turn right there and that the house is on the opposite side. And true enough I do find a white porch with a red door. I recognize that as familiar and ring the bell. So here I am; "I knew the way" all right, despite my bad memory for street names and numbers.

You have never been there before, but you have armed yourself with a street plan. So you unfold it at the station exit. "This round dot must be Cranberry Park Station. This widely spaced pair of lines with a dotted line between them must be the street before the station with trolley buses on it. Yes, there is something that looks like a church on the other side. It must correspond to that cross on the plan. Lilac Gardens is the third side street opening off that broad street on the right, going left from the station." So you turn left, cross two side streets and reach the third corner. There you see my grocer's shop which happens also to be a sub-post office. You therefore find it marked "P.O." on the plan at which you glance. Thus reassured, you turn right. And as soon as you can find two legible house numbers, you identify our friend's house by simply counting. So your safe arrival proves that you too "knew the way."

Of course you did not really need to unfold the map after reaching the station. You could have studied it in the train and translated the information you gathered from it into a simple rule for action: "Turn left from the station and then take the third street on the right." You could memorize this rule and follow it without further reference to the street plan, a wretched flapping thing that is sure to tear in the wind. (Of course there is a wind tonight as we are in England!) In either case your claim to knowledge of the way was better founded than mine.

The "knowledge" I was using was strictly private and therefore misnamed. In fact I was behaving in much the same way as the rat who learned his way out of the maze in the last chapter. When a certain stimulus was presented to my vision—the church on the far side of the broad street—I reacted to it in the manner that had proved satisfactory on a former occasion. Similarly the learned reaction was repeated in response to the stimulus of the grocer's shop and pillar-box on the third street corner. Electronic machines behave just as intelligently and can be credited with at least as much "knowledge."

You, on the contrary, had no memories of past experiences to guide your steps. You were guided instead by other people's experience which had been put at your disposal in the form of a map. The latter just condenses in a *symbolic* form the actual observations and experiences of the persons who made the map. For several generations surveyors and draughtsmen, employed by the British Government, have in fact been engaged in triangulating, measuring and plotting London and the rest of Britain for the Ordnance Survey and revising periodically earlier results. The latest edition of this official map served as the basis for the street plan you bought. But local authorities, transport undertakings and some commercial firms may also have been consulted and contributed information for inclusion in the plan. It is therefore very much a social product, the result of co-operation between a number of individuals and corporate bodies. The street plan embodies and condenses some of the observations these various contributors have severally made and publicizes them; it makes them accessible to you and other purchasers of the plan so that you can use them to find your way about London and its suburbs. I mean to say, the Government surveyors and the agents of co-operating institutions have noted down and expressed in symbols what they actually saw with their eyes, walked over, handled—what in fact they perceived with their private sense organs.

Of course not all the information thus gathered by surveyors and other observers is communicated to you in the map. They have not included in the plan the heights of the buildings along the streets, their architectural style or lack of style, their use as shops, dwellings, offices, hotels, the smells issuing from some, and a thousand other details which one or another must have noticed. These would just confuse you and distract you from your purpose of finding your way to a given house from a known station. To meet the needs of persons like you the map maker has indicated the directions and lengths of streets and sometimes their relative widths, but not the quality of the pavements, the presence of trees nor as we said, any characters of buildings fronting the streets. Such features, which some of the surveyors must have noticed and may have recorded, have been deliberately ignored in the published plan. To introduce at once a technical term very popular among philosophers, the map maker has *abstracted* from the total picture observed, collected and reported by his collaborators, certain selected metrical and geometrical aspects of the region mapped. This abstract information, embodied in the map, suffices for your purpose when you bought the map; from it you can deduce the simple rule for action quoted on page 14.

But had your purpose been to enjoy—or not—late Victorian suburban architecture or to learn about the distribution of social classes in London suburbs, the street plan would have been no use. For the first aim, photographs might have been more helpful; they show lots of details, omitted from the map as irrelevant to the main purpose for which it is made, bought and used. On the strength of such omissions we say that maps are more abstract than photographs. Even an air photograph, though it does show, like the plan, the directions, relative lengths and widths of streets, includes in addition features considered superfluous in maps. Once again the map is more abstract even than an air photograph. But this abstractness, the omissions from the map do not diminish, but enhance, its value as a means of conveying information that can be used for a specific purpose.

The street plan embodies or expresses an aspect of knowledge of London. By studying it—this sheet of paper in your hands—you, as we say, imbibe this knowledge. It somehow gets "into your head" as it was once "in the heads" of the collaborating surveyors and draughtsmen. Then "in your head" it is turned into a rule for action ("turn left, cross the main street and then turn right at the third corner"). And this rule is projected "out of your head" when you carry out its directions by walking—but of course not onto the map's streets on the paper, but onto the London streets that are represented on it. Thereby you prove to yourself that the information contained in the map was correct, the knowledge expressed in it was true; the map was a true and faithful representation of the London suburbs within its own confessed limitations.

The map of London, constructed and used as just described, can with a little ingenuity be turned into a first-rate philosophical puzzle—indeed into three distinct puzzles. Firstly, how did London or a street therein—two rows of substantial buildings of bricks, stone, concrete and wood, spread about in three dimensions on either side of an equally substantial paved strip—ever get "into the head" of the map maker? Then how can the map maker get this knowledge of London "from his head into yours"? And thirdly, in what sense does this two-dimensional street plan covering eight inches of flat paper correspond to a three-dimensional city covering eight square miles? The first question is a particular case and a vulgarized version of the "epistemological problem" itself. This whole book is an attempt to answer it or rather to translate it into a form that might be answered. Answers to questions two and three are essential to a reformulation of the first. The third turns out to be the easier and will occupy Chapter III. But first it may be well to emphasize by another concrete example the contrast between knowing and remembering.

My successful journey to my friend's house was not a very good example of the use of memory. I merely remembered the correct responses to certain stimuli when they were presented. The street with the church on the other side, the grocer's shop and pillar-box, the red door on a white porch had become *cues* to which I reacted when I encountered them. But memory can do much better than that. One can memorize a whole process and reproduce it without waiting as I did for cues to be presented. The guardian of a certain ancient monument can recite to tourists quite a good explanation of the ruins he is showing them. But if his monologue is interrupted, he is at a loss how to proceed; he has to start again at the beginning and repeat all he has already recited before he can go on. He does not really "know" the building's history, and so understand what he is saying. He has just learned off a set of words which he can repeat by rote.

We used to start learning geometry in this way. We learned by heart or memorized some definitions and the proofs of a couple of theorems. If we could repeat the theorem and proof verbatim, we were said "to know Theorems I, II, etc.," of our school geometry book. But unless we and our teachers were unusually stupid, we soon realized that it was quite unnecessary to memorize nine or ten lines of print. We began to grasp the meanings of the terms used and to understand the argument set out in print. We recognized that it had a pattern, though we did not yet know it was called a "logical pattern," and saw that each step in the proof "followed" from the one before. Then once we had mastered the first step or two, we could find the next for ourselves without looking at the printed text and certainly without bothering to memorize it. Having a poor "retentive memory," I found this a lot less trouble than trying to learn another page of print by heart. Though my performance in class may have been less ready than that of more conscientious pupils who obediently learned the exact words of the book, I maintain that I "knew" the theorem better than they! Thanks to my appreciation of the logical pattern I knew a step in the proof as set out in the book that I had never read and so could not remember.

In a sense, indeed, you can know things that no one has experienced, and so that no one remembers. If you know the route of a ship or the path of a projectile, you know not only where it is now, but where it will be in ten days or ten seconds—unless of course it be sunk or deflected in the interval. Armed with this knowledge you can send a cable to catch the ship in Cape Town or—with luck—intercept the projectile. In a word, if you know a pattern, though what you have before you is incomplete, you can complete it *in imagination, imagine the* remainder. After all, from your study of the street plan in the train (page 14), you knew what you ought to do on leaving the station, you could forecast your actions and imagine yourself performing them. Of course, if you found the street "up" and even pedestrian traffic diverted, your forecast would have been wrong and you would have to change your plan. You would not, however, say that the map was wrong or gave you false information, but simply that it did not give you enough. Knowledge always has in it an element of foreknowledge in that it justifies some expectation, but expectations are still liable to be deceived, however well founded.

III.

Patterns, Correspondence and Communication

THE street plan used as an illustration in the last chapter exhibited of course a pattern. Its correspondence with the pattern of London streets is just an instance of the correspondence of patterns. This conception is crucial for the subsequent argument so that it must be examined in detail. But the correspondence of maps involves some peculiar complications so it will be well to begin with a simpler example.

Empty your matchbox on the table at random. You have before you an amorphous chaotic heap. No doubt all the matches have a certain thickness and length; they are all made of the same sort of pale wood, and above all we hope they will all ignite. But as a heap they have no structure; they form no pattern; they are disorderly. Now take three matches from this disorderly pile and arrange them end to end. A marvellous transformation ensues. Collectively the three matches now form a pattern, the geometrical figure called a triangle, and each has become an element in this pattern, a side of the triangle. Thereby they have jointly and severally acquired a new property. The triangle can *correspond* to any other equilateral triangle, whether made of matches, or lead pencils or telegraph poles, and each match *corresponds* to a side of this other triangle.

Plane geometrical figures, like triangles, are very simple patterns and to that extent offer easily apprehended examples. More complicated patterns exhibit the same properties, often in an enhanced degree. All communication is based on the correspondence of patterns. The Morse code of dots and dashes provides a very simple and familiar example of the kind of pattern used in long-distance communication. A message transmitted in the Morse code is in fact a very simple instance of what is technically termed a *time series*. The dispatching instrument can emit only long or short buzzes, but can emit either indiscriminately. Theoretically therefore any long buzz is just as likely to be followed by a long buzz as by a short one, and so on. Hence the probability of any particular sequence arrangement of longs and shorts is always less than one. The longer the succession the more improbable it grows—i.e., the less likely to be the result of pure chance. Each repetition of the same sequence multiplies the improbability. To repeat this in symbols = = and = • are equally probable; the probability of = = is said to be 1/2 and so is that of = •; the symbols = • • are more probable than = • • • =; the probability of = • being repeated twice in succession is half that of = • occuring at all, i.e., 1/4.

Drumming aimlessly on the table or hammering nails in a board you may produce a random series of long and short taps, but it will probably exhibit no discernible order or pattern. But you have all read stories about the prisoner confined in a dungeon by the Gestapo or the NKVD. He notices such a tapping noise and then suddenly he realizes that there is a recurrent rhythm in the noise, a most improbable repetition of the same rather unlikely combination of long, short, short. He is excited to recognize a familiar pattern, a key signal in the Morse code. (Unlike the present writer, the imaginary prisoner has always happened to have served as a telegraphist or something equally improbable.) He thereupon starts tapping out the combination of longs and shorts appropriate for a response. And so he establishes communication with the victim in the next cell. They expatiate at length on the iniquities of Hitler or Stalin and then proceed to plan their escape. The ordered patterns of shorts and longs constitute messages and convey information through the cell walls from one prisoner to the other. Note by the way the amount of information conveyed by each such message is inversely proportional to the probability of the pattern constituting it. (For instance a pattern whose probability is 1/4 conveys twice as much information as a pattern with probability 1/2.)

The message patterns used in ordinary talking and in telephony are of the same kind but far more complicated and enormously more unlikely. All are time series; all are four dimensional; all can be resolved into the components—length, amplitude, velocity.

Such patterns can best be compared to the waves you see in liquids, but that does not help very much; wave motions are much more complicated than most people imagine and can only be described with the aid of very abstruse mathematics that I do not profess to understand. But without appealing to the intricacies of wave mechanics, the reader may believe that the possible patterns are enormously varied and immensely complicated so that the probability of any one is exceedingly small. And the mystery of a telephone message can easily be expounded.

Consider what happens physically when A, a jam manufacturer in Glasgow, rings up E, his agent in London, four hundred miles away. A makes certain patterned movements of his lungs, mouth and vocal chords. These set up (1) waves of sound in the air which, impinging on the transmitting instrument, cause (2) its diaphragm to vibrate. Its vibrations (3) make and break an electric circuit causing pulsations of current to pass along the four hundred miles of wire (I use the old metaphorical expressions simply to economize words). Each pulsation (4) magnetizes an iron core round which the London end of the wire is wound. So the electromagnet attracts and repels another piece of iron attached to a diaphragm in the receiver. This diaphragm (5) thus vibrates, just as that in the transmitter did, and by vibrating sets up again (6) waves in the air. They in turn impinge on the diaphragm of E's ear and its sympathetic vibrations excite auditory nerves in E's head.

I have deliberately simplified my account by omitting minor though necessary events, but the process as described sounds complicated enough. Simplifying further by ignoring for the moment psychological, neural and muscular events between A's speaking and E's hearing, there have intervened waves in the air, vibrations of a diaphragm, "pulsations of electricity" in a copper wire, magnetization and demagnetization of an iron core, vibrations of a second diaphragm, four hundred miles from the first, and a second set of waves in the air! Air, diaphragms, copper wire, magnets are all for common sense quite different things easily distinguishable by sensory perception. All indeed move, but each in its own way. So we can distinguish spatially or otherwise six sets of movements between the utterance of the message through A's lips and its reception by E's ears. Yet all are equally involved in the message's transmission. Only the pattern of movements remains constant throughout the whole transaction. The pattern alone preserves its identity or remains *invariant* throughout all the changes of medium—in air, in "electricity," in magnetism, in vibrations of metallic diaphragms or membranes. The pattern of air waves corresponds to the pattern of diaphragm vibrations, to that of electric "pulsations," and so on. And each element in the air-wave pattern corresponds to an element in the next and that all through the six versions of the pattern. The pattern in fact constitutes the message transmitted. But the pattern consists in the *relations between its parts or elements.*

We are accustomed to think of patterns as two dimensional —the designs woven on carpets or painted on walls. But the patterns used in communication are, as we said, time series; they are four dimensional. But it is possible to petrify such a pattern. The time dimension can be removed without destroying its order, the relations between its constituent elements. That is what is done in recording on a Dictaphone or gramophone. Replace the make-and-break attached to the diaphragm in the transmitter by a needle so arranged as to scratch a moving strip of waxed tape or a rotating disk. The pattern thus becomes fixed in three dimensions, the time dimension being projected onto the axis of the tape or wound round the spiral on the disk. You can of course restore the time dimension and make the message audible once more. All you have to do is to "play the record" on the appropriate machine. You can thus prove to yourself how far the pattern remained invariant despite the change of dimension.

But a sound pattern can be made visible as a three-dimensional pattern in much the same way. All you need do is to replace the recording needle by a pen and the waxed tape or disk by a sheet of paper. The sound waves made by your voice when thus projected into one plane look like this: ᴧ/᷍ᴡ/᷍ᴧᴧ

Anyone can see that the pattern is very complicated, very improbable and so very distinctive. The chances are quite negligible that random movements of your vocal cords or similar noises or the struggles of an insect that has fallen into the ink could produce just that track. Of course any particular element by itself—say ᴧ/᷍ alone—might be meaningless "noise." It is only because it thus occupies this position in the series and exhibits precisely this relation to the rest that we know it must correspond to a particular word or syllable in the spoken message.

Not only does a pattern as thus defined retain its identity when one dimension is removed, it may still remain invariant though one of the remaining dimensions be varied. Speak the same message into two recording machines, the tapes of which are running at different speeds. On the slower machine the whole pattern will be spread out more widely; the intervals between crests and troughs will be longer and the angles will be less acute. But the crests will preserve the same relative positions on both tapes and the heights of, and intervals between, each will keep the same proportions. So the two patterns and the several elements in both still correspond. Both records when played at appropriate speeds will return the same audible message.

It will be convenient to digress here to illustrate the last point by another example. Tree-ring patterns are used by American archaeologists for dating prehistoric, pre-Columbian ruins. The significant patterns are not, however, the visibly outlined figures that are plainly revealed when you slice a tree trunk horizontally, but the more abstract patterns constituted by the varying thicknesses of the annual growth rings. The thickness of each of these is determined mainly by the abundance or inadequacy of the rain that fell during the year the ring was formed. Now, in a single tree the pattern thus defined must be the same throughout its whole height. But of course the trunk, and consequently each ring, is thicker near the roots than at the top, and the actual contours of a cross-section with its component rings are likewise liable to vary at different levels. Still more will these features vary between different trees in the same area though the significant pattern, determined by fluctuations in the annual rainfall, must remain the same, since all the trees considered are presumed to have enjoyed the same climatic conditions. So neither tabulated measurements of the actual thicknesses of consecutive rings nor photographs of cross-sections of trunks will reveal the correspondences that concern archaeologists. For that they reduce the complicated pattern reproduced by photographs to a more abstract pattern showing only relative thicknesses. It is a sort of wavy curve rather like the speech track on page 26 in which the crests represent the thickest rings and the troughs the thinnest. Thus plotted the correspondence between the curves from the same tree at different heights and from neighboring trees leaps to the eye at once. But if you were in doubt, there is a mathematical formula for "goodness of fit" to determine whether or how far they really do coincide.

Now, tree rings may reveal something more than the local fluctuations in precipitation. Comparing a series of such curves, covering a number of years but drawn from different regions, despite very conspicuous local divergences in detail from year to year there may emerge correspondences in a more abstract pattern. That is to say, among the many ups and downs a few troughs and crests may appear recurring at long but equal intervals and of proportionate heights on all the curves. Joined up in different coloured ink to form a new curve, they will exhibit corresponding patterns that are more abstract in as much as all local annual variations have been abstracted or omitted. Perhaps the abstract curve reflects a sunspot cycle or some equally global phenomenon.

Tree rings illustrate how a pattern may be compounded of, or analyzed into, two or more simpler patterns. Of course this compounding of patterns is familiar to all musicians and is conspicuously heard in most classic compositions. (Musical patterns are termed themes or even tunes.) The principle will be found important in later chapters, but is so plain that further elaboration is needless here.

The equilateral triangles formed of matches and telegraph poles showed that a pattern may retain its identity though the size be changed (may remain invariant in respect of magnitude); the telephone call proved the same for changes of medium. Tape recordings proved how a pattern may persist though one dimension be varied or even removed. But if we can subtract a dimension without destroying a pattern or abolishing correspondence, can we not add one? I find it convenient to extend the term pattern to embrace wholes the identity of which depends upon the mutual relations of their parts even when the relevant relations are neither spatial nor temporal. And at least metaphorically one might term the sort of relation that holds the parts together—e.g., function—a fifth, sixth or nth dimension as the case might be.

In a machine that which integrates the multifarious parts is *function*. Of course the parts are all arranged in a spatial order and thus do constitute a three-dimensional pattern. But this arrangement may be changed and the whole spatial pattern transformed without in the least impairing the identity of the pattern of the machine as such. Take an ultra-simple case. Ford and most English automobile manufacturers produce cars equipped with either right-hand or left-hand drive. So in two 1954 Ford "Pilots," steering column, gear levers, brake pedals and many other parts may differ in position; to look at, the two chassis are emphatically not the same. But both work in the same way; the steering column in the one corresponds to that in the other—in function but not in position. In this sense I shall talk of functional correspondence and functional pattern though some writers would prefer "structure" to "pattern."

In living organisms function is more obviously decisive. In the foetus each embryonic organ corresponds to some counterpart in the adult in function despite absurd divergences in size and even in relative position. In the same way it is meaningful to speak of the correspondence between the lungs and other organs of a whale and those of a man or any terrestrial mammal despite still greater differences in size and arrangement. The essential thing is not to mistake patterns for geometrical figures or to confuse correspondence with congruence or similarity.

We are now in a position to begin suggesting answers to the questions raised on page 17 with reference to your successful use of your street map of London. The two-dimensional eight-inch map of London streets corresponds to the actual layout of the city in almost the same way as the triangle composed of matches on page 21 corresponded to that made of telegraph poles. Almost, but not quite. For in the first place your map, like both the triangles, is strictly in one plan—flat—whereas London is hilly and, as part of our globe's surface, slightly convex. But for your purposes it has been possible to abstract from the enormously complicated spatial pattern presented by London a simplified geometrical pattern by ignoring irrelevant features that would show up for instance on an air photograph. With this abstraction your map corresponds reasonably well. No doubt the rather irregular lines of shop, house and garden frontages bordering the street on either side have been for convenience represented by parallel straight lines on the map. Still, in direction, length and even width the map streets correspond geometrically to the real streets. Again the street corners are shown as angles whereas some are really rounded off. And so on. The general pattern is preserved despite these abstractions; the several figures outlined on the plan are geometrically similar to the blocks of shops and houses separated by streets.

Secondly, the plan does not present a self-contained pattern or figure, like a triangle, but a selected part of a larger figure. Its relation to the latter is indicated by its orientation.

Thirdly, your map shows features which as such do not figure in the geometrical pattern abstracted from the complexity of London; the underground station and the bus route would not show up at all on an air photograph. Your map shows stations, churches, bus routes by ⊖, + and . . . How do these marks correspond to actual buildings and routes? Physically the circle with a stroke through it is not the least like the entrance to an underground station. The cross might to some extent reproduce the cruciform plan of an Anglican or Roman Catholic church, but the church you and I both noticed was Wesleyan and so not cruciform. Buses do not leave a line of dots down the centre of a street, and, if they do leave a trail of oil and grease, it is indistinguishable from that left in other streets by trucks and private vehicles.

No, these marks are *symbols;* they correspond to features on the streets of London only by *convention.* Map makers have agreed among themselves to use these marks to stand for stations, churches, bus routes. In buying the map you tacitly became a party to the agreement and assented to the convention. You had to learn what such marks meant, and to help you an "Explanation of Signs" is attached to the map. By studying this you were initiated into the conventions of what might be called "cartographic society." Having been thus admitted to membership and initiated, you can share the information collected by and for its members. Its conventional symbols are one of the vehicles for conveying this information to you.

Symbols are indeed the most familiar and most useful means of communication. Map symbols, though conventional, are relatively easy to understand. Each such symbol refers to or "means" a single definite class of objects— stations, churches, bus routes. Such objects are in turn capable of *ostensive definition;* that is to say, you can point to a station or church with one hand and to the symbol with the other instead of, or as well as, relying on a word or verbal formula to explain the symbol. In practice of course this "ostensive defining" was done for you in early childhood with respect to the words "station," "church." The written word explains the symbol adequately to you, but if you had been a foreigner it might have been necessary to point to an instance.

Even so the meaning of the symbol on the map is not fully elucidated by the explanatory note. You were able to identify the ⊖ on the map with Cranberry Park Station where you alighted because of its *context*. Its position on the plan, its relation to other stations on the Piccadilly Line which you had passed, to the street with buses running on it and to the Wesleyan Church were essential factors in defining the meaning of even this very simple and unambiguous symbol. Both features are common to all symbols; their meanings are always determined both by convention and by context. Symbols have meanings only by agreement between members of a society, but their meanings are defined only by the symbols' relations to other elements in a pattern.

The conventional, and therefore social, character of symbols may be used to distinguish them from signs or signals. And this distinction may be illustrated from the example just considered. In using the map to find your way, you had to interpret symbols. To me, on the other hand, the church on the other side of the street, the grocer's shop on the corner were just *signs* or at best signals to cross the street or to turn right. Their meanings for me I had indeed learned, but by my own prior private experience. In some town plans, stations and churches and similar features are represented by pictures instead of conventional symbols. If the likenesses are reasonably close, the plan's user will be able to discover the meanings of such pictorial representations in the light of his own experience without referring to any written explanation. They are signs rather than symbols. The interpretation of signs normally depends on purely private experience and is by no means a peculiarly human "faculty." Pavlov's celebrated experiments with decerebrated dogs proved that the sound of a bell rung on oft-repeated occasions before the presentation of food became in time a "sign" of food and stimulated the appropriate reaction—secretion of saliva—just as effectively as the smell, sight or taste of actual food. Sign behavior such as is exemplified by Pavlov's dogs or by "me" on my way to a suburban dinner party is always learned behaviour. It is therefore based on previous experience and utilizes stored information thus acquired. Yet the experience is usually private and the information need not be, and seldom is, communicable. In fact sign behaviour can be fully explained in terms of the conditioned reflex as set out on page 32.

In conclusion let us restate the suburban dinner-party example in the terms that have been explained in this chapter. I found my way to my friend's house because I had been there before and had looked where I was going. Though I could not describe in advance what I had done on previous occasions, when I actually saw certain buildings and streets, I recognized them as signs and signals to execute certain muscular movements. The information that invested them with these "meanings" was, however, private to me and incommunicable.

You, on the other hand, made use of social knowledge, communicated to you through a map. You could use the map as a vehicle of such knowledge and a guide to successful action because you learned and accepted the conventions laid down by society as to the meaning of map symbols, and because the pattern on the street map corresponded to the geometrical plan of the suburban streets. Thanks to the contexts of certain symbols on the map, you were able to identify on it a particular church and station. From the information thus acquired "in your head" you deduced a rule for action and applied it. Acting on this rule you objectified the theoretical knowledge derived from the map and thus incidentally proved to yourself the truth of the information it conveyed. For normally we do not study street maps just for fun or derive aesthetic or other enjoyment from looking at them. Your use of the map was the normal one—to find out how to get to a destination. It provides another illustration of the thesis, advanced on historical grounds in Chapter I, that knowledge is useful in practice and practical in function.

IV.

Symbols and Their Meanings

TURN now to the second puzzle: How did the information contained in the map get "into your head"? Plainly, this puzzle is of the same kind as that raised by the telephone call from Glasgow to London (page 24) and its solution must be found along the same sort of lines. The message spoken by A was heard by E four hundred miles away, because a pattern of physical events remained invariant and retained its identity through six transformations or changes of medium. In its last version, as sound waves emitted by the receiver, the pattern or message did get into E's head. But the phrase "in his head" is being used in a literal and in a metaphorical sense. The latter sense is what is really intended in the puzzle, but the literal sense is the more readily understood. In hearing the words uttered by A in Glasgow and repeated by the receiver in London, the pattern of sounds literally did get "into E's head." The sound waves set vibrating the tympanum (eardrum) of E's ear, and its vibrations stimulated or excited a number of neurons in E's brain—to be precise, in his cerebral cortex. These neural excitations presumably formed a pattern that replicated the pattern whose invariance we have already followed through a series of external vicissitudes. We cannot describe this pattern even as accurately as the corresponding pattern in the copper telephone wire, though it is almost certainly not a geometrical pattern; at least in the case of vision it is known that seeing a round object is not the equivalent of a circle of stimulated neurons being formed in the cortex. Let us just call it a "neural pattern" and remain content to know that the neural pattern in E's head corresponded to the pattern of sound waves in air, diaphragm vibrations and electric pulsations outside his head.

So the physical (including therein also physiological and neural) aspect of communication can be explained or described quite satisfactorily. But the message was made up of words, and its content, the information communicated, consisted not in the physical sound of the words, but in their meanings, the "ideas" they conveyed. The metaphorical sense of the puzzle is thus equivalent to "How did the sound pattern, happily introduced into E's head, have the same meaning there as it did when produced by A?" By analogy the answer must be that the meanings or ideas in turn must form a pattern corresponding to that formed by excited neurons, air waves, electrical pulsations and all the rest. But this bald statement is not very illuminating and indeed may seem to mean nothing at all. To elicit some meaning from it will require two chapters and some apparent digressions. In the first place meanings may provisionally be treated as attributes or properties of symbols. I am unable to discover or even imagine a meaning floating about detached from any symbolic embodiment or vehicle. Then symbols are sensible observable physical things or events while meanings are usually considered spiritual or psychical.

Let us begin by examining the observables—symbols and especially words, the symbols of language. Words were in fact the symbols used by A in communicating information to

E and successfully understood by E. Plainly, the transmission of the message would be pointless unless the words meant the same to A and E. We have tacitly assumed that they were not using a secret code, but both spoke English. This language they did not invent; they had not personally had to agree on what the several symbols should mean, as they would have done in concocting a code. Both had learned to talk English from their parents and schoolmasters; these had taught them how to pronounce the words and what meaning to attach to each. A and E took a language ready-made for them by society and used that language as their means of communication, just as they used the telephone network and instruments that had likewise been provided by society. So the symbols employed had the same meanings not only for A and E but for all members of a much larger society, for all English-speaking persons, alive or dead.

In this, as in other senses, meanings are universal and transcendent. Before A and E were born the same words had the same meanings, and they will continue to bear them when A and E are dead, as long as anybody at all speaks and understands the English language. (It is convenient here to ignore quite substantial changes of meaning that many words notoriously do undergo in time and have undergone even in my own lifetime.) The meaning thus transcends, not only each utterance of the word, but also each individual speaker —A, E and all the rest of us.

Meanings are transcendent and universal in other senses; all symbols, like words, which bear conventional meanings are general and abstract. This is most easily seen in the case of names, even proper names. In naming anything you ignore all the individual peculiarities that distinguish and indeed constitute the substance of any empirical object—any object that can be perceived by the sense, felt, touched, seen, smelt, tasted, heard; you mean such general characters as it shares with other objects to which you apply the same name. Thus any perceptible cow is grey, brown, dappled . . . a certain size, standing in a byre or grazing in a field, mooing or more quietly chewing the cud. In calling it a cow, however, you ignore all these individual features in this cow; "cow" does not mean any particular one of them, though none of them is incompatible with the word's connotation. I find it con-venient to term any individual animal to which the word "cow" is applicable (i.e., which it can denote) an *instance* of the symbol's meaning while I term "the *idea* of cow," all that the word can embrace. The word "means" both, but it is the *meaning* as *idea* that is universal. The idea of cow lacks all the individual peculiarities that distinguish every empirical cow.

The meanings of even proper names are in this sense general and abstract. Gordon Childe today is 61.8 years of age, moustached and writing this book in a hotel near Naples. Thirty years ago he was clean-shaven and studying the ruins of Mycenae in Greece. And so on. But the name means equally all these very different appearances and yet no single one more than any other! The idea that a name means, always transcends any and every instance of what the name means. The same is equally true of other words and symbols though not always so easy to demonstrate.

But ideas as meanings are universal in a third sense. The identification of a perceived object as the meaning of a sym-bol is implicitly an assertion that the object exists independ-ently of the percipient's perceiving it. Naming *objectifies,* and that in two senses. Consider first an infant learning to talk. You point to an object which you both can see and say, "cow." It is quite likely that on the first occasion there was no permanent object for the infant, only an undifferentiated and rather incoherent mass of sounds, smells, colours, shapes, simultaneously besieging his senses. He is helped by the pointing and naming to pick out from this mass a constellation of visual, auditory and olfactory sensations that hang together as adjuncts, attributes or, if you will, meanings of "cow." The symbol forms as it were a nucleus round which these sensible qualities can cluster; it emphasizes their isolation from the general background to stand out as an "object." By a repetition of the process of naming and pointing, the name "cow" becomes firmly attached to the constellation of sensations which thereby is recognized as a persistent durable grouping—a permanent object. When it recurs, the infant will cry "cow," not of course to inform you of anything, but to consolidate its own experience.

But even if the foregoing account of objectification be correct as far as it goes—and I think the Gestalt school of psychologists have given some grounds for disputing it—it is not the whole story. The blind, deaf and dumb girl, Helen Keller, seems to have learned to distinguish objects before she was taught a sign language. But she describes vividly how delightedly excited she was on discovering that "everything had a name." Why? Not surely because this showed her that things existed independently of her; for that she seems to have appreciated already. Her delight was caused rather by the discovery that they existed also for other people, in fact for a society of which she was a member. So she could share her experiences with them and benefit from theirs in as much as the objects experienced were common to her and them. And this too the child discovers in learning to talk.

In this sense naming a thing objectifies it and asserts its

existence. Whatever is named exists for the society that names it and uses the word. "To exist" is here used operationally. The last assertion may be restated as follows: Members of the society that name a thing and use the symbol will take account of the named thing in their actions and will adjust their behaviour to it. Whatever ghosts mean to you or me, they mean things which members of illiterate and of past societies and some members of our own fear, and to avoid or placate ghosts they will perform or abstain from certain overt actions. Even sceptics in denying the existence of ghosts are admitting their existence as ideas—delusions they say—in the heads of some of their fellows. Naming objectifies the named in the sense that society believes in its existence and acts as if it existed. In this lies the creative power of names: *in the beginning was the word.*

Words do create what they mean, but only for the society that uses them. Now, society may be mistaken, and the word may perpetuate an error. Indeed words and other symbols all too often mislead to delusion instead of guiding to knowledge. The trouble is partly due to the duality of the meaning of "meaning," as Ogden in particular has shown in a well-known book. Suppose A's message had been: "A hailstorm at Blairgowrie has destroyed the raspberry crop. Buy me all you can in Kent." The message refers to things, places, events and situations in the external world in which A and E live. "Hail," "raspberries," "Blairgowrie," "destroy," "buy" mean or refer to such physical events and things which Ogden calls the *referents* of the symbols. The same symbols, however, refer also to what I have called ideas in A's and E's heads which Ogden calls "references." The latter, as such, are not capable of being perceived by A's, E's, or anyone's senses as the referents were and will not be quite identical for A and

E. It is not, for instance, the hail as a meteorological phenomenon that interested A, but hailstones battering raspberry bushes. Yet these references, just as much as the referents, will affect men's conduct—in particular, the actions of A and E.

All symbols have meanings, but many have no referents in Ogden's sense, and some logicians seem inclined to doubt the respectability of such words. What is the referent of $\sqrt{-1}$ or "electric current" or "democracy"? There can be no referent to $\sqrt{-1}$, but the symbol is anything but meaningless. Mathematicians find this "imaginary number" invaluable in completing an immense variety of calculations, and the results obtained by its use can still be successfully applied in practical life. No electric fluid flows along a copper wire, but the Electricity Board measures the current I consume and charges me for it. There is no agreement as to what "democracy" means, but men have been, and still are, willing to work very hard, to pay heavy taxes and even to die to defend or establish "democracy." Words may refer to actions as well as results, and the doing is just as reputable a referent as the thing done. Operations, even when performed in the head, are just as good referents as more physical and external processes. From this point of view division (say of 189 by 7) is no less respectable than the dissection of a corpse by a student's knife.

Again the meanings of all words and many symbols have both an imperative as well as an indicative aspect. Symbols are used not only for the communication of information, but also for the stimulation or restraint of action. After all, A did not send an expensive telephone message four hundred miles just to inform E of a curious meteorological event near Blairgowrie, but to instigate him to buy raspberries to cover the loss. We have argued on historical grounds that knowledge is practical in function so we must insist that all words are not only symbols but also to differing degrees signals for action.

Of course it is very confusing that all words look so alike when their legitimate meanings and functions may diverge so widely. Formally and grammatically "cow" and "cause" are indistinguishable, and philosophers have got themselves into frightful tangles by talking of causes as if they were just like cows. It may be still more misleading when a word which is primarily imperative is used as if its meaning were descriptive. "Communist" once meant a person who had joined a political party with a clearly stated political and economic program and was thereby committed to work for the realization of this program. It is applied to an old-fashioned liberal, not of course to describe his political and economic views which are diametrically opposed to Communism, but as an opprobrious epithet to prevent his employment. "Fascist" is abused in precisely the same way in Communist circles! Undoubtedly many fallacies have been introduced into thinking by an abuse of language, but the abuse consists in general not in using words that have no referents, but in mistaking the category to which the meaning refers—e.g., in confusing things with operations or wishes with facts. Before elaborating this point another characteristic of linguistic symbols needs to be noted.

The meanings of the words of a language, like those of the symbols on a map (page 30), are defined by their *context*. A word quite by itself, with no context, really has no meaning. If in a general buzz of conversation through a lot of noise I just catch the single word "fire," it really does not mean anything to me. So if I chance to see the word "bull" written on one of many scraps of paper in a waste-paper basket, it means nothing. To acquire a meaning any such sound or mark must have some context, but this need not be other words, i.e., a sentence. A cry of "fire" in the night is liable to mean quite a lot, but it generally has a context; it breaks the quiet abruptly; it is generally accompanied by sounds of scampering about, often by a smell of smoke or an unexpected red glow. In this context "fire" has a lively imperative meaning; it is a call to immediate action. So if on a country ramble I see BULL painted on a gate, its situation gives the word a meaning. It warns that there may be a bull in the next field. So, if I am wise or timid, I will not pass through the gate but change my route.

The meaning of a word is so largely determined by its context that the same sound can be used with several totally different meanings without giving rise to serious ambiguity. In English the sound *tu* has three quite distinct meanings that are actually represented in writing by three differently spelled words. But if in a foreign thermal resort like Bad Gastein you hear someone say loudly, "*Tu* hot baths," you are hardly ever in doubt whether an attendant is indicating the way to the baths, or a would-be client is ordering baths for himself and his wife, or thirdly, a disgruntled bather is complaining of the excessive heat of the baths he has just sampled!

What is true of speech is equally true of writing. In the cuneiform script, used by the Babylonians and Assyrians and employed for diplomatic correspondence by most ancient Oriental states in the second millennium B.C., the same character may stand for two or three distinct sounds and also for a whole word with yet another phonetic value. In practice this polyphony, as it is called, never caused any inconvenience, as the value of the written symbol was always adequately determined by its context. Bad handwriting can be deciphered by invoking the same principle. Recently I received a letter in reply to one of mine from a very distinguished French colleague. The words are scarcely divided, the several characters run together and are almost indistinguishable; any particular squiggle might by itself just as well stand for *r* as well as for *e* or *s!* A Frenchman, who did not know what the letter was about and was not familiar with all the technical terms used, abandoned the attempt at decipherment. But knowing the sort of things a reply to my own letter was likely to contain and most of the technical terms and names involved, I succeeded in uncovering even such an odd word as *faunique* from the execrable scrawl that disguised it!

Most words indeed have several meanings, though not as discrepant as *to, too* and *two*. A pocket dictionary lists synonyms for each meaning of the original word. In reading English a foreigner can then get the meaning by seeing which of the synonyms best fits the context where he has met the word, but he will not get much help in using it himself. A larger dictionary gives quotations illustrating the correct use of the word in each meaning in a suitable context.

The last three paragraphs could be condensed into the simple statement that words and characters are symbols precisely because they serve as elements in patterns. Such elements, from the side of a triangle upwards, can correspond to something only because of their relation to other elements in a pattern. The relation of a symbol to its meaning—to its reference and to its referent—is one of correspondence while the pattern in which symbols are elements is a context.

V.

Ideas as Meanings

THE real information transmitted by the telephone call from Glasgow to London was not the time-series pattern that remained invariant through all the transformations described on page 24. The content of the message was not the symbols, the words spoken by A and heard by E. It was rather the symbols' meanings, the ideas they conveyed. But E understood the message, A's meaning. So the pattern of ideas in E's head must have corresponded to that in A's, and accordingly to the pattern of air waves, diaphragm vibrations, electric pulsations, etc., that intervened. But not in quite the same way as the sound waves and electrical pulsations corresponded. To make quite sure, consider the next transformation suffered by the message. E translated it into (bad) French! He cabled M. O., the great fruit merchant of Havre: "Un tempête de grêle vient d'anéantir la raccolte de framboises à Blairgowrie; en achetez toutes que vous puissiez en Normandie." This message does correspond to that sent by A and heard by E, but how? The words do not look or sound similar. When spoken, they can also be expressed as a time series. But the time series, the pattern of sound waves made by the French words, does not correspond to that produced by the original English words. The correspondence is in meaning only. O can understand A's message because the pattern of ideas represented by the French symbols corresponds to that meant by the English symbols. But what is a "pattern of ideas"?

We have called the meaning of a symbol an idea. From that definition of this very controversial term, a whole series of characteristics can immediately be deduced. (1) Ideas are quite unsubstantial; there is no stuff ideas are made of; so if spirit be the opposite of matter, ideas are really "spiritual." (2) Yet there are no ideas apart from symbols expressing or embodying them. (3) Symbols are material objects or events —waves in the air, excited neurons, marks on paper. But such objects and events by themselves have no meanings, except when understood by a member of a society. (4) An idea is not tied to any particular physical vehicle; the same idea can find expression and be the meaning of many physically different symbols. (5) Ideas exist only in heads, but are not tied to any particular head; they can be communicated to all members of the society that sanctions the conventions of symbolism. (6) Ideas are objective because, and in so far as, they exist for, or in the heads of, a whole society of intercommunicating persons. (7) New ideas originate with individuals, but become objective only in so far as they are communicated to, and approved by, some society. (8) Symbols as such are artifacts and acquire their meanings by social convention, but all artifacts may be vehicles for, and are expressions of, ideas. (9) Ideas form patterns, but these are not like the geometrical patterns woven in a carpet nor the time series used for their communication.

In composing this book I have several times—in my bath or when out for a walk—felt as if I had got a really bright idea. But when I come to write it down, I find nothing put down. I expect many of my readers have experienced like disappointments. Well, we were mistaken. There was no idea. For an inexpressible idea is just nothing. An ineffable truth is neither true nor false; it too is nought. To "have an idea" you must find or make a symbol to express it. You will nowhere find disembodied ideas existing on their own, not even in the gray matter of a brain nor among the valves of an electronic machine. The spiritual idea can be born only when its material vehicle is ready for it.

But the vehicle need have no occupant. By itself no symbol can have a meaning nor convey an idea; it must be understood by someone and used as a symbol by someone. Words are physical waves in the material air generated by very complex movements of bodily organs. These waves and movements alone interest a phonetician, and for him "ávabígró-kumintáp" might be just as informative as "Oh! for a draught of vintage . . ." But the first string of sounds has no meanings, and we, like most people, are more interested in the ideas expressed by words than in their phonetic peculiarities. But this book full of words contains no ideas unless somebody reads it. Ideas are not qualities of words or other symbols, like size and shape. All the words in the dictionary have no meanings while the volume is closed. The mere spatial collocation in parallel columns of sets of printed characters does not invest one column with meanings. So again the characters of the Indus script (used in the Indus Valley about 2000 B.C.) have no meanings, because no one can decipher them. We believe they had meanings once—to the nameless Indus people who invested them with conventional meanings and used them for communicating ideas. But that society has perished, and the tradition which maintained their conventions has been broken. The idea, expressed by a symbol, exists only in the heads of those privy to the convention that made the symbol a symbol.

But the same idea can be expressed by several different symbols. Thus E translated "buy" by "achetez"; he hoped the word would convey the same idea to O as A's word "buy" conveyed to him. Conversely the same symbol may be used to express several different ideas. There is in general no one-one correspondence between symbols and ideas. Again it was shown on page 42 that the meanings of symbols are determined in a large measure by their context. Now the normal contexts for words are sentences, and it is in such that ideas are conveyed. But though sentences can be analysed into distinct words, their meanings cannot be so exactly divided up into separate ideas; it is often debatable how much of a sentence was needed to convey a single idea!

The relation of thinking to language may be considered as a corollary to (3) and (4). Reasoning has been described (page 12) as "operating with symbols in the head." Similarly a behaviourist has called thinking "sub-vocal talking." This description, I must confess, agrees very well with what I think I can observe by "introspection" as going on in my head in the preparation of the present or any other argument. It seems to involve the postulate of mental images which figured prominently in all psychology textbooks fifty years ago, but are now rather unpopular. They would be faint reinstatements of the heard sounds, seen letters, etc., of symbols and words—perhaps feeble excitations of the cortical ends of sensory nerves not stimulated in the sense organs proper. In that case they should be detectable by neurologists, and if they are, images will doubtless reappear in the textbooks. Even so, combination of images of symbols will not give an entirely satisfying account of thinking if only because there is no one-one correspondence between symbols and ideas.

But while words and other symbols convey or mean ideas only in heads, the ideas are no more the private possession of any particular individual than are the symbols that convey them. The ideas contained in Mr. A's message were not peculiar to him but were familiar to E and O and hundreds of other orchardists and businessmen not only in Britain and France but all over Europe. All these ideas A had learned, as well as symbols with which to express them, from the society in which he had been brought up. Only because E and O had similarly imbibed the same ideas, could they understand A's message. To an African clerk, just arrived from Nigeria who had never seen a raspberry nor heard of Blairgowrie, the message meant nothing when he heard it repeated in E's office. In fact the message implies a world in which not only do places like London, Glasgow, Blairgowrie, Kent, Normandy occupy specific positions in space, but in which too raspberries grow, are bought, sold and turned into jam. To understand the message it was therefore needful not only to have been initiated into the conventional meanings of the symbols in which its meaning was expressed, but also to know, i.e., to have in one's head an ideal representation of, the world to which it applied. So ideas are objective both because, like the meanings of symbols, they are common to all members of society whose behaviour may be modified in reference to them, but also because what they imply exists for society in the same degree. Ideas exist only in heads. They are objective only if they exist, not in your head or mine alone, but in the myriad heads of a hydra we call Society. Thus ideas really exist outside your head and mine.

Many existed before we were born and will still exist when we are forgotten.

That is not to say they exist in a mystical empyrean "tranquil and exempt from coming to be or passing away" as Plato implied. Ideas exist only for, or in the heads of, a society. Society is of course made up of individuals, but transcends each and every one of its members. Individually each member of society is mortal, but society outlives all its members by many generations. Yet human societies too are mortal. Ideas likewise are mortal; they survive as a rule only so long as the society which knows, understands and expresses them. Prehistory and history are littered with the skeletons of extinct societies. The clerks who wrote the Indus script, the stone carvers of Easter Island have perished utterly, and with their languages have died all the ideas those languages expressed. The Sumerians who dominated Mesopotamia in the third millennium have likewise vanished; their language was extinct for two thousand years till last century Assyriologists learned to decipher Sumerian texts written on clay tablets in the cuneiform script. But long before that decipherment, ideas, elaborated by Sumerians, had been transmitted to us through the Babylonians, Assyrians, Hittites, Hebrews, Greeks, Etruscans and Romans. For luckily ideas can leap political and linguistic frontiers.

Of course an idea may die "a natural death" too. The society that cherished it, instead of itself perishing, may abandon or reject the idea as false or unnecessary. Thus ideas are doubly mortal. But if ideas die, new ideas are born. I hope this book may give expression to and suggest to its readers some new ideas. If so, they will have been produced from my head, like Athena from the head of Zeus.

For new ideas are born, that is, first given expression, in

individuals' heads and only an individual can devise the symbolic vehicle to convey it. But no idea lives unless it be accepted, cherished and sustained by some society, some group of individuals that transcends and outlasts the originator and all the rest of its members. For ideas are not born until they are expressed, and normally men only express ideas in order to communicate them to someone else. Doubtless we can imagine a hermit expressing his ideas in words in imaginary conversations with his deity. Presuming the latter too to have been imaginary, the hermit's uncommunicated ideas would not exist historically unless subsequently communicated to real disciples who should understand, approve and propagate them. So if an inventor died without leaving specifications, models or even apprentices to reproduce his inventions, neither the inventor nor his inventions would exist for the historian of science. Ideas exist only in heads, not in a single solitary head, but in the intercommunicating heads of a society.

Ideas have so far been treated as if they were expressed solely in conventional symbols like the words of a language. But all such symbols are artifacts, the results of deliberate human action. No natural process will produce sound waves consistently ordered in a time series to be heard as, for instance, "deliberate human action." Still less will a natural force produce the graphic symbols, the typescript characters that transcribe such sounds. All such symbols are produced by the cunning of some human organ; "artifact" means just "produced by artifice." Then, in the light of page 46, "the excogitation of a new idea" is equivalent to the invention of a symbolic vehicle to express it. The history of mathematics abounds in examples of the limitation of mathematical thinking by imperfections of the available symbolism and notations.

So Hogben and many others have pointed out how the progress of Greek arithmetic was blocked at every turn by a clumsy numeral notation based on the system of beads on an abacus (counting frame). With the diffusion by the Arabs of the "Arabic" (really Indic) numerals came a liberating revelation; not only because it expedited arithmetic operations, but because it facilitated the expression, and so the discovery, of hitherto unrecognized properties of numbers. Or take "Pythagoras' Theorem" or rather its converse: "A triangle is right-angled if the square on one side is equal to the sum of the squares on the other two." Preliterate barbarians seem to have used triangles with sides in the proportions of 3, 4 and 5 for laying out rectangles. They "knew" one case of Pythagoras' Theorem but not the universal property of all right-angled triangles that it enunciates. About 1500 B.C. Babylonian clerks drew up a list of triads of numbers—3,4,5; 5,12,13—bearing the required relations (Pythagorean ratios). They may be said to have "known" that any triangle with sides in one of these ratios would be right-angled. They certainly possessed no mathematical symbolism with which to express the general theorem nor does any verbal enunciation of it survive. So presumably the Babylonians did not "know" the proposition. Only the Greeks invented a geometrical symbolism (it has been called geometrical algebra) that enabled them to state—and also to prove—the famous theorem and so really to know it.

But if symbols, devised as vehicles for ideas, are both artifacts and tools, tools—artifacts made for immediate practical use—may yet express and embody ideas. Who will dispute that an electronic valve or an aeroplane is the material realization of an idea? Doubtless in either case the "idea" was first expressed in the conventional symbolism of a blueprint so that you might call the product the referent of the blueprint while the idea was its reference. This objection, however, will not hold good of the more difficult inventions made by nameless inventors in preliterate societies. Take the first plough ever made—if an archaeologist could recognize it (page 2). Did "the idea of plough" wait to be born till the village elders had approved the device and solemnly given it a name of which "the idea of plough" then became the meaning (reference)? Of course not. The idea was born as and while some ingenious cultivator was fitting together bits of wood that thereby became share, beam and pole, and yoking to the result a pair of oxen; by these physical actions he was expressing, as well as realizing, the idea.

Every artifact thus expresses and also realizes an idea. At the same time a tool is also to some extent a symbol, in so far as it suggests its function. The plough not only embodies and exemplifies an idea, not only incorporates the technical skill of its maker, but calls to the ploughman to use it. A constituent of the idea of plough is ploughing. And so with any tool; its idea embraces the purpose for which it has been made.

Let not the reader be unduly dismayed if he has not yet understood what ideas are made of and how they form patterns. Light is said to be propagated as waves and for most purposes behaves like waves. But waves of what? The Aether of Space was invented to satisfy materialists who asked that question. It has now been dismissed as an unnecessary and undemonstrable postulate. But we go on successfully dealing with light waves; we measure the wave lengths, we arrange to discount their interference and so on. Let us treat ideas in the same way. The author has described some of their "prop-

erties" but always on the assumption that one of them was
to form patterns. For patterns were necessary to explain or
to describe by analogy how information "gets into heads
from outside" (page 43). The word "idea" has been introduced mainly to answer the inevitable question "patterns of
what?" and is thus disconcertingly like "the Aether of Space."
I shall nevertheless continue to use the symbol with the
proviso that it may in the end turn out to have no referent.
After all, though the term "pattern" too be used metaphorically, it must always imply parts—elements, moments, components, or members—which are related one to another.

It follows indeed from the previous paragraphs of this
chapter that the elements of ideal patterns are very unlike
the mutually exclusive parts of the spatial patterns that suggested the metaphor. Ideas cannot exist by themselves like
the threads of a carpet (page 45) or the matches that made
up a triangle. Nor can their relations in the pattern they
compose be external as are those of the sides of a geometrical
figure or of the tesserae in a mosaic. The original analogy
was really a very poor one. Time series come nearer what is
wanted; in a symphony the several notes, played simultaneously by different instruments, are heard as one sound,
and distinct themes are blended in a single harmony. Yet the
several notes can be distinguished by appropriate instruments
and the themes disentangled by a trained ear. Functional
patterns in a machine or organism are in some ways more
helpful analogies. We may find the behaviour patterns of
societies better still. But if explanation be to describe the
strange in terms of what is familiar and amenable to control,
the last analogy will not be very useful. Such warnings, deduced from characters attributed to their constituents, must
precede the attempted description of the pattern of knowledge.

VI.

Knowledge as a Social Construction

FOUR preliminary chapters have been introduced to familiarize the reader with my usage of several terms that may have seemed unusual and are certainly ambiguous, but to define which would have involved either a circular argument or the introduction and explanation of still less familiar terms. Only after this preparation can I venture to offer the reader even a provisional definition of the book's first title. What I propose is the following: Knowledge is to be an ideal reproduction of the external world serviceable for cooperative action thereon. To amplify each term:

(1) "Is to be" because no science claims exhaustive knowledge and also because knowledge as here understood can never be complete nor final.

(2) "Ideal" that is "in heads," but not in your head or mine alone (page 48) but "in the heads of society." It was superfluous to include the word "social" in the definition since its implication in "ideal" has already been demonstrated. In the sequel I sometimes use "conceptual" as equivalent of "ideal."

(3) Re*production* is used to emphasize that knowers do not just receive impressions and passively reflect them as mirrors do. They produce a pattern from them.

(4) Yet *re*produce, in as much as the elements and pat-

tern are given in experience and derived from the external world. It must therefore somehow correspond to that world.

(5) External world because (mainly) outside heads. I use this term as the counterpart of ideal in preference to real to avoid suggesting that ideas are unreal. But where there is no ambiguity I shall say "reality" for variety.

(6) "Serviceable in action" is just a reassertion of the "practical character" of knowledge as deduced on historical grounds on page 9.

(7) All distinctively human action is co-operative. Even war involves a kind of co-operation! That is why a Nilotic tribe prefers to make war upon the people most like it! I could not write this book without the (unconscious) co-operation of the hosts of workers who have collaborated in making and distributing the typewriter and the paper on which I write, to say nothing of all the philosophers, scientists and psychologists whose books I have read and whose ideas I have borrowed, often unconsciously or without acknowledgement. Our daily bread reaches us only through a vast co-operation of farmers, millers, shippers, bakers, and retailers, not one of whom need ever have heard of the other nor of the ultimate consumer who in turn at best knows personally only the retailer. And right back to the Ice Age the palaeolithic mammoth hunter only got his dinner by co-operating with his fellow clansmen in a collective hunt, since alone he was no match for a mammoth! (Compare Chapter VIII.)

From the definition thus expanded, a series of deductions can be drawn. Knowledge is derived from experience. Data for its ideal reproduction get from the external world "into heads" through sensory perception. But sense organs are parts of individuals' bodies, and sensations are private to individuals. So common sense—like too many philosophers—assumes naïvely that a man, like any other organism, secures his knowledge of the outside world—of his environment—as percepts through his senses. But this is less than half the truth. Only a tiny fraction of the external world in which I act has ever come within the range of my sense organs, and in that fraction I perceive little more than what my society has taught me to perceive.

What I notice is very largely determined for me, not by nature, but by nurture. What I perceive is conditioned not only by the characters of my sense organs and of the stimuli —the sounds, smells and so on proceeding from the external world—that excite them, but also by the training I have received from society in their use. My sense organs are being continually besieged by a disorderly rabble of stimuli. I cannot attend to all; I must make a selection. A few loud noises, flashes of light, or disgusting stinks force themselves obtrusively into perception; the rest are consciously or—more often —unconsciously selected, and in either case the selection is socially prescribed to a larger extent than most people recognize. An archaeologist, a grazier and a botanist will all see different things when walking over the same tract of grassland—the line of a Roman road, good (or bad) pasture for sheep, varieties of Graminaceae including a rare species! For the botanist and farmer there just was no Roman road; they had not been taught, as the archaeologist had, to notice or interpret the straight strip of short parched grass with patches of conspicuously luxuriant herbage running parallel on either side.

In the Australian bush a black tracker can detect traces that whites seem incapable of perceiving. The black's eyes do not differ physically—nor physiologically nor neurologically

—from those of white's as the noses of bloodhounds differ from those of men; under laboratory conditions the black's vision would be found no keener than a white's. But from his early youth the aboriginal had been trained by his elders to observe minute disturbances of soil and vegetation—a displaced leaf, broken twig, etc. Such marks are equally visible to black and white, but have been invested with meaning in the hunters' lore of aboriginal Australian societies.

You and I, Messrs. A, E and O can communicate about, and co-operate in, one world, not only because the same stimuli from a common external world affect—or might affect—our sense organs, but also because a common social tradition has taught us what to perceive. What lies quite beyond that tradition may pass unnoticed. Pacific Islanders who made and used seagoing canoes, when first visited by European ships, were delighted with the cutters and their gear, but showed no interest at all in the ships themselves or their engines. These just did not fit into the pattern of the islanders' "world."

Secondly every individual's world enormously transcends the limits of his private experience. I have never been to Japan or Mexico, but I send letters to colleagues in those countries and quite often get a reply. Other members of my society have visited these countries and have made public their experiences there. Their observations have been communicated to me and all members of the society to which I belong in lessons, books, lectures, maps and timetables. No one has ever seen an atom nor directly perceived one with the aid of any other sense. Since the discovery of radioactivity it has become possible to photograph individual helium atoms, and in Wilson's cloud chamber the path of an ion is made visible. But after all what you see on the photographic plate or in the vacuum tube is only a sign. Only in virtue of the physicists' interpretation does it mean an atom. And long before the Curies' discovery or Wilson's invention made atoms visible in this sense, physicists and chemists had inferred their existence and operated successfully on these imperceptible objects. They had for instance been weighed. So crystallographers can describe precisely the positions occupied by each imperceptible atom in a molecule that is still far too small to be perceived by the eye or any other human organ of sense even when aided by the most powerful microscope or other magnifying instrument, and can reproduce the invisible patterns thus formed in visible scale models.

Disease germs or bacilli are visible under a strong microscope. But if I were presented with a culture on a slide and a focussed microscope, I still should be unable to distinguish a typhoid bacillus or indeed any other. Yet, like most Europeans and Americans today, I unhesitatingly submit to injections to ward off the attacks of these unseen foes. Like Mexico and atoms, bacilli exist for our society; some members of that society have experienced proof of their existence and published their findings which have accordingly been incorporated in the ideal world of my society. The world in which I plan to operate and to co-operate with others is not the world which I have perceived privately and experienced individually, but the ideal world of knowledge englobing the collective experience of all members of my society.

In the seventeenth century English society believed firmly in witches. Hardly any Englishmen indeed could claim to have seen a witch. But they accepted the statements of the experts who did claim such experience with the same credulity and, I confess, on as good grounds as you and I accept the advice of bacteriologists. Seventeenth-century society believed in witchcraft—that is, acted as if witches existed—and imposed that belief on its members, just as twentieth-century societies believe in bacteriology and by compulsory vaccinations and inoculations compel their members to act in accordance with their prescriptions. We call the former belief a superstition. But as long as society really did believe in witches and its members habitually and deliberately acted on that assumption, we must admit that witchcraft was comprehended in that society's "world of knowledge."

That is of course just an admission that human experience is fallible, human knowledge incomplete. The ideal reproduction of the external world in society's heads is not, and in fact never can be, an exact reflection of that world: It must indeed in some measure correspond to the latter, and we hope that, since knowledge is cumulative, our reproduction corresponds better to the external world than did our ancestors' of three centuries ago. To justify this hope the bacteriologist might point to the empirical evidence available to public inspection that verifies his hypotheses—to the bacteria swarming on the microscope slide and so on. His demonstration would not make the least impression on a resuscitated Englishman from the seventeenth century nor on a contemporary believer in witchcraft brought in an aeroplane from his village in the African jungle. He would do better to point to the mortality figures. The decline in the death rate from typhoid and cholera is an argument that even the Negro witch doctor must accept; it shows to anyone that burning garbage is more effective than burning witches! The sole criterion of the correspondence with reality of one society's world of knowledge that the member of another society can understand or accept is the success of actions based on rules deduced from it.

Our knowledge in the twentieth century we may hope corresponds better to the external world than that applied by seventeenth-century witch burners. But our ideal reconstruction is certainly not a complete copy or reproduction, and indeed for three reasons cannot aspire to be such. In the first place the function of knowledge is ultimately practical —to provide rules for action. For that a full and complete reflection of the external world would be useless; an abstract chart would be more convenient. Your map of London in Chapter II was more serviceable than an air photograph to guide you to our dinner party; it omitted details, irrelevant to your purpose, and also marked features that a camera in an aeroplane would miss. A plastic three-dimensional model would have been even less helpful to you; the intricacies of the complex reality of London, copied in every detail, would merely have confused you. Even the physical pattern of London is too immensely intricate to provide easily rules for finding one's way about. Yet it is only the bare skeleton of the life of the city. The external world is enormously complex; to find our way about it we need a simplified "map," to speak metaphorically.

The construction of such a metaphorical map is a co-operative enterprise far more than the construction of the street map of London. The data are of course provided by individuals in both cases; they are the messages received by the participants from outside their heads through sense perception. But, as we have just been insisting, each individual can perceive only an infinitesimal fraction of the whole, and not every private perception is relevant. Each may make an infinitesimal personal contribution but no more. The collection of data has been going on ever since Man as such emerged upon the Earth. The construction of a known world, an ideal reproduction of the external world, is a cumulative process, and the result at any time represents the pooled experience of mankind.

Perhaps the most distinctive peculiarity exhibited by Homo sapiens alone among the animals is the habit of communicating his experiences, the information he receives through his senses to his fellows. Without such communication men could never have co-operated, and without co-operation men could not live at all; the mammoth hunter of the Old Stone Age depended on co-operation for his dinner as much as a twentieth-century city dweller. Admittedly a lot has been lost in the process. Regularly communication only takes place between members of the same society, and mankind is, and apparently always has been, divided by language, kinship or politics into many societies. Yet today men can and do communicate across political and linguistic frontiers while prehistory and history show that intercourse between distinct societies has always been going on if never before as fast or extensively as now.

Societies in the sense of tribes, nations, political states and speech communities may perish, but much of the information that they have accumulated as a world of ideas outlives them and is handed on to successors in a larger society. Some indeed, like the Indus people of the Bronze Age, appear to have dissolved without communicating to their successors any of the information they had accumulated and pooled. But this appearance is almost certainly misleading. No doubt many of the ideas expressed in the Indus script have perished with those who understood the symbols' meanings. But archaeology has proved that some of the craft lore, i.e., the technical knowledge, of the Indus civilization, survives. To this day, for instance, village potters in Sind are using the same distinctive techniques and utensils as their nameless predecessors used four thousand years ago; in other words these contemporary craftsmen are applying the rules for action deduced from the same technical knowledge as that applied by members of the prehistoric society. Moreover there are grounds for believing that ideas were transmitted from the Indus civilization to the Babylonians as manufactured goods demonstrably were. In the case of the Babylonians and Egyptians, the Hebrews, Greeks and Romans, the continuity of tradition from antiquity to the present is familiar. The transmission has not been effected only, or even mainly, by their surviving writings. The decipherment of the cuneiform and hieroglyphic scripts in the last century just served to show how many basic elements in our world of ideas, "in the mind of Western Christendom" to use a cant phrase, had originated in Babylonia or Egypt and had been passed on to us through the Greeks and Hebrews long before direct written messages became available. In the same way it could be shown how much information was communicated to Europeans by the pre-Columbian inhabitants of America and the aborigines of Australia. But for further evidence of the pooling of ideas I refer the reader to my Pelican, *What Happened in History.*

"Pooling" is a handy metaphor, but like all metaphors, it has its limitations and, when applied to the construction of a map and still more of a world of knowledge, may be even misleading. Information is not just poured into a map by the several contributors into whose heads information had similarly been poured from the outside world through sense perception. On the contrary the raw data, received as isolated messages by the contributors, have been sifted and shaped and then fitted together to form a new coherent pattern in the map. So the raw data for knowledge, received as private experiences, are not just poured into a communal reservoir, but are co-operatively shaped, fitted together and built up into a structured edifice. The component experiences no more automatically come together to form a pattern than do the scraps of painted plaster that have fallen from the collapsed walls of a ruined building.

A colleague of mine has recently been reconstructing the fresco adorning the walls of a room in a Roman villa at Lullingston in Kent. When the villa was destroyed, the painted plaster collapsed in crumbling fragments, and the small bits were strewn chaotically all over the floor. When he started, my colleague had no idea what design the unknown artist had painted on the wall sixteen hundred years ago, and hardly any of the scraps of plaster would join owing to their friable edges. Yet he eventually discovered the pattern though many pieces have totally disintegrated! The patterns of the external world have equally to be discovered, but they are enormously more complicated and come to us in a still more fragmentary condition.

An orderly world is not presented ready-made in perception, but only in disconnected bits from which to construct such. *Eine Welt ist uns nicht gegeben, sondern aufgegeben,* as Kant put it. The pattern or patterns must be discovered. That there is a pattern has been assumed. It is the necessary, if undemonstrable, postulate of knowledge as here defined. It is the essential condition for any correspondence between the "ideal" world "in heads" and the "real" world "outside." For only patterns and elements in patterns can correspond. So the external world must be structured and patterned;

otherwise there could be no ideal reconstruction to correspond to it. This is precisely what is meant by Hegel's famous dictum, "The Real is rational and the Rational is real." Only if the Real is patterned, is it knowable at all. There is no sense in talking or writing about an unknowable Reality. If such existed, it would have no practical significance for anybody. No one could adjust his behaviour in relation to it. Throughout this book it has been maintained that the function of knowledge is practical. In fact mankind's biological success in surviving and multiplying affords empirical evidence that useful knowledge of the external world—of man's environment—is attainable. And that is the only justification that could be advanced for the postulate enunciated by Hegel.

Admitting that the external world has a pattern or structure, then the ideal reconstruction, here termed knowledge, must exhibit a corresponding pattern. Here the reader must again be reminded that the patterns of which we are speaking metaphorically comprise not only the two-dimensional patterns on walls or carpets that originally suggested the metaphor. The expression is in fact habitually applied to four-dimensional patterns, to the time series used in communication and discussed at length in Chapter III. Anthropologists write about "patterns of culture," psychologists and sociologists about "behaviour patterns." If their writings constitute useful contributions to knowledge, such patterns must be components of the pattern of reality. We have in fact spoken metaphorically of n-dimensional patterns.

Remember too how patterns can be analysed into more abstract component patterns (page 28) and simplified by the omission of one or more dimensions. So the four-dimensional pattern of a speech could be reduced to a three-dimensional one on a gramophone record and even to a two-dimensional graph (page 25) and still retain something of its identity. It was by a similar process of reduction that the map maker simplified the physical pattern of London by abstracting one dimension of space. Regarding the pattern of reality as n-dimensional, the process whereby natural scientists—let us say geologists, chemists and atomic physicists—discover progressively more abstract, but at the same time more general, patterns may be regarded as an analogous process of reduction.

Reduction of dimension of course involves impoverishment, and the abstract pattern thus obtained corresponds less completely with that of the external world. But the success of action guided by the more abstract pattern—for instance the success of physicists in designing nuclear weapons and canalizing for human use nuclear energy—provides operational proof that the correspondence has not been disturbed and that the more abstract patterns actually are components of reality's infinitely richer pattern. The pattern scratched on the gramophone record, being as such inaudible, is plainly poorer than your speech and does not correspond to it completely. In this case full correspondence can be obtained by restoring the fourth dimension, in other words by playing the record.

Now the rich, complex pattern of reality must be at least four dimensional; it is not simpler than a time series. But since a time series is an essential component of the full pattern, at no moment is the pattern complete. The pattern of the external world would be no more complete now at 20 hours, 31 minutes and 12 seconds on July 31, 1954, than is the tune of "Home Sweet Home" complete after two and a half bars have been played. This, I confess, is a metaphysical assertion rather than a statement of the known as defined on page 54, but I hold it to be a legitimate deduction from communication theory which has vindicated in practice its claim to be a branch of knowledge. The use of "time" implied here is defended further. Accepted, it supplies a second reason why knowledge cannot be complete.

There is yet a third reason: not only is the object of knowledge, the pattern of the external world, itself incomplete, but also in so far as it has been completed, it is so rich and complicated that twenty-two million generations of men just have not had time fully to discover it—or should we say, to extricate it from the minute incoherent fragments in which it is presented to private experience. Remember that for most of those 500,000 years all men, and even now most men, are entirely absorbed in the primary business of keeping alive and propagating the species with the aid of the scraps of knowledge they have inherited from the social store. They had to be content with just enough knowledge to do that—what to eat, how to make fire and use it, which kind of stone to use for tools and so on. A very few were adventurous enough to try new foods, four or five inventors of incomparable brilliance hit upon or devised new methods of kindling fire, an unique genius discovered copper smelting. Out of such experiences and experiments, publicized, has slowly grown by cumulative accretion the world of science.

If the external world be patterned, the ideal reproduction we call knowledge must of course likewise be patterned, however much the pattern be reduced and simplified. Only a patterned world of ideas in heads can correspond to a patterned reality outside them. Now we have been unable to find ideas apart from the symbols of which they are meanings, and ideas can only be communicated by means of these symbolic vehicles. A world of ideas must therefore have a symbolic basis, and knowledge, being communicable, must be expressible. An ideal pattern must then also be a pattern of symbols. The normal vehicles of communication are the conventional symbols of language, including mathematical symbolism. Other kinds of symbols may convey and express ideas. But knowledge as here defined does not find expression in the symbols of art or of religion any more than in dreams, the private symbols of "the Unconscious" (a mythical entity imagined, but successfully used, by psychoanalysts).

If knowledge as a pattern of communicable ideas is *ipso facto* a pattern of symbols, we are not thereby committed to the assumption that the physical pattern made by the symbols—I mean the time series of sound waves or the spatial arrangement of characters scrawled or typed on paper—must as such correspond to reality. On the contrary the fact of translation (page 47) refutes any such suggestion. Nor for the same reason is the pattern required definable in terms of the grammatical relations of the verbal symbols; grammars differ as much as vocabularies. On the other hand the flow of words in the succession of symbols in every language does seem to correspond to the flow of ideas, as observed by psychologists, and to the course of events experienced in the external world.

If the pattern of the external world be at every moment incomplete and since the pattern of ideas "in heads" is incomparably less complete, it might be objected that knowledge is unattainable or at least unusable in practice. Neither objection is, however, really valid. Admittedly the correspondence between fragments of patterns can never be so close as that between complete patterns. Part of the activity of "reproducing" the external world consists just in the endeavor to improve the correspondence by completing the pattern *in imagination*. But after, all messages from the external world are received in perception already patterned so that parts of reality's pattern are perceived as such by private human beings and surely by lower animals too. The information thus received is in turn communicated to others by patterned messages.

The second objection is more serious. The function of knowledge is practical, to provide rules for action. But action takes place in the future and follows the deduction of the guiding rule. Yet only the past or at best the present can be known. So reality being a process and its n-dimensional pattern comprising time as a component, it will have changed before action ensues, and so the knowledge on which the rule was based will no longer correspond to it. To preserve the correspondence and be able to act successfully on the external world men have to anticipate the pattern in imagination. In so far as mankind has survived and multiplied, men must be able to do precisely this. Their many failures show that they do not always anticipate correctly.

VII.

The Categories as Constructional Tools

TO EXPLAIN the method of filling up gaps in experience and anticipating future developments, I must have recourse to another analogy. I propose to compare the reproduction of an ideal world of knowledge to the rebuilding of an ancient monument, say a ruined Saxon church, by a team of archaeologists, architects and craftsmen. Most of the material is there already: stones tumbled from the walls, window frames, capitals, voussoirs, roofing tiles are lying about the site, chipped and battered in disorderly heaps. These it is planned to re-use and replace in their original positions. But pieces are missing; some stones have been carted away, others have crumbled into dust, but many are just buried in the debris and will come to light as this is removed and replaced in its former position. Immediately the missing parts will have to be replaced—at least temporarily—by substitutes of concrete or similar material suitably shaped. Some of the wall foundations and column bases are still in place and suggest the outline of the ground plan, but, as work proceeds, fresh wall footings may be exposed under tumbled stones and may impose modifications of the suggested plan. The archaeologists know from other churches of the period that survive in better preservation, the general design and superficial appearance of the complete edifice. The details are, however, totally unknown; no one knows how many windows were on each side nor exactly how the roof was constructed in this individual instance. That they hope to find out on the one hand by recovering the mouldings and springers, on the other hand by experiment. For they plan by actual building to find out by trial and error how, within the limits set by their general knowledge of this church's plan and the common design of such churches, the surviving fragments can be fitted together into a stable edifice. As it proceeds, the work will reveal gaps caused by missing parts and these will have to be filled by substitutes. A scaffolding will be needed to support window sills or capitals till the actual walls have been raised high enough to receive them and at the same time to guide the masons and others co-operating in the enterprise. The scaffolding is in fact the skeleton of the design, provisionally outlined by the architect in the light of the archaeologists' deductions. But it must be flexible since the provisional design may have to be modified to accommodate the surviving fragments which must all be fitted in, to ensure the structure's stability, or in the light of discoveries made in the course of the work.

Let the surviving pieces of the ruin represent the perceptual data in our ideal reproduction called knowledge, and let the church as built in A.D. 950 stand for the structured external world it must reproduce. Then, just as in the church the missing parts had to be replaced by substitutes shaped like surviving structural elements, so the gaps in pooled experience must be filled with symbols, expressing ideas imagined on the model of ideas, already socially approved and objectified. As the architect had to anticipate the design that the original and substitute pieces are to form and to lay out a scaffolding accordingly, so knowers must anticipate the uncompleted pattern of reality in imagination, using partial patterns already known as a frame to support their hypotheses. But this frame must be flexible since hypotheses must be modifiable in the light of practice.

The imagined ideas or fictions, used as substitutes for empirical data, are all too familiar. They are expressed by symbols which, as often as not, have no referents and so cumber all languages with words that may have no meanings and yet look deceptively meaningful. But many are, or have been, really serviceable, and all were probably once necessary. A whole host of eminently respectable symbols used in science, as in everyday life, were produced to express imagined meanings, and have only later acquired referents as a result of experiments, i.e., actions, that could not have been planned without their aid. Others that were likewise useful for that purpose have been discarded for terms whose meanings correspond better to reality. Other symbols were invaluable for the communication of information and for description and are still found convenient for that purpose even though they prove to have no referents and even after better descriptions have been found. Many electrical phenomena, particularly conduction, were found to be quite satisfactorily described in the terms applicable to flowing liquids. The term, "electric fluid," current, or shortly, "electricity," was thus coined to form the grammatical subject in descriptive sentences which yet conveyed useful information, i.e., knowledge. Though we know now that there is no fluid flowing along copper wires so that the symbol strictly has no referent, the term is as we saw already still found useful in practice, and its reference remains a convenient idea.

Psychoanalysts have created a whole pantheon of mythical entities—the Unconscious, the Censor, the Ego, the

Libido . . . It is doubtful whether these symbols have any better referents than $\sqrt{-1}$. But like the latter, they are convenient and useful in communication and in action. With their aid, observed phenomena can satisfactorily be described, and rules for action have been deduced that have undoubtedly relieved or cured neurotic and psychotic patients.

"Centaur" may once have been just as useful. It was no more a creature of the imagination than the "electric fluid," and no less. As the idea of an "electric fluid" imagined as water was created to fill a gap in experience, so was that of combined man-horse. It may have served a prehistoric peasant society, unfamiliar with the use of horses for riding, as a convenient symbol to denote the first mounted warriors it encountered and to communicate information about these unwelcome strangers. But by Homer's time the centaur was already a mythological creature. In this case it is not only the failure of humanity in three thousand years to find an instance of "centaur" empirically that has induced society to abandon the word as a symbol describing reality; a fuller appreciation of the biological and psychological characters of men and horses shows such a combination to be inconceivable. In other words, once the connotations of "man" and "horse" respectively are adequately understood, it appears that "man-horse" can have neither connotation nor denotation; "centaur" is literally meaningless with neither reference nor referent.

It is needless to dwell on the hosts of demons, ghosts, spirits, magic forces that have plagued humanity in the past. All, like the electric fluid or the Aether of Space, were created by imagination to fill gaps in experience as substitutes for missing structural parts without which the rebuilding could not proceed and rational action would be impossible. None were created out of nothing; all were imagined on the analogy of authentic perceptual data though those data may have been distorted by illusions and delusions. All have been, or still are, objective in as much as a social convention has invested the symbol with meaning, and some society by incorporating the word in its language has imposed the idea on its members. They are, or were, objective too in that society, believing in the reality of the fiction, behaving as if it did form an element in the external world and obliging their members to act accordingly; otherwise co-operation with their fellows is impossible. If a society's ideal reproduction of the external world be built too largely of imagined substitutes without referents, it may be impossible to correct its errors as long as the society holds together; for its members will be literally incapable of perceiving data that do not fit into the design of the edifice! But the trouble is more often due to a too rigid scaffolding—to a misuse of categories.

A *category* connotes the outline of a pattern, the kind of relation holding between elements in a pattern that is itself presumed to be a component pattern of the external world. If not perhaps under this title categories are familiar to every reader—I mean "space," "time," "causality," "substance," and so on. Each denotes a way in which empirical data are supposed to hang together to form a pattern and the kind of pattern thus formed. They are clearly very abstract ideas indeed. I have compared them, not very happily I fear, to the scaffoldings used in rebuilding the Saxon church to guide the builders and to support the walls during their re-erection. They follow the plan of the church as disclosed by the surviving wall foundations, but, it will be remembered, these were only partially exposed and the clearance of the debris may reveal a rather different plan. At the same time the scaffolding might enable the builders to anticipate where part of an arch or other structural element might go provided suitable supports for it were subsequently found and fitted.

It is just such an anticipatory function that a category should serve in building up a serviceable ideal reproduction of the external world. It is used in the belief that this outline at least of the latter's pattern will persist and preserve its identity in the interval between knowing and doing. The total pattern is changing at every instant, but component patterns may continue to follow the same outlines without practically significant deviations. In so far then as the ideal reproduction follows such a pattern's outline, it will for practical purposes continue to correspond to the pattern of reality. For instance it is plausibly assumed that the constituent parts of the external world are and will be arranged spatially or "in space" though of course the actual arrangements of such parts are ever changing. This assumption yields the category of space. So causality assumes that there will be a pair of events, A and B, such that B "invariably" follows A.

Philosophers have maintained that the categories are necessary preconditions of knowledge, not derived from experience but given *a priori,* and existing eternal and immutable in their own right. If the first claim means that the external world exhibits a pattern, it is just a restatement of what was said on page 63 and must be endorsed. If it mean that knowers must somehow know the outlines of patterns before they can know their contents, it would seem to invert the sequence. Yet just this is implied in the assertion that the categories are given *a priori.* Finally the alleged immutability of the categories is rebutted empirically by the history of thought; categories have changed during the course of written history as will be illustrated shortly. On the other hand, these philosophers are right to this extent that the categories are not given *as such* in private experience. Patterns are perceived, their abstract outlines have to be discovered. Perception is a private affair; the discovery of the general outlines of patterns contained therein is the result of social co-operation, and it is society that objectifiés the categories as thus discovered. These points must be amplified and clarified by two concrete examples—space and causality.

For Kant space and time were the *a priori* preconditions not only for knowledge, but even for perception, the raw material of knowledge. And from the concept of space all the propositions of Euclid's geometry could be deduced *a priori*. This curious belief was due in no small measure to an atomistic psychology assuming that the several senses—sight, touch, etc.—supplied discrete messages to the (individual) Mind—a fiction—that then somehow combined and arranged them in a pattern. It is the merit of the Gestalt school of psychologists to have shown that experience does not present a lot of disconnected bits but a pattern; objects are apprehended as forms (*Gestalten*). Men, and presumably animals and even insects, behave as if they perceive things and events as in front or behind, above or below, to right or to left, before or after.

Nevertheless this private space, perceived as occupied by things, by the objects of action and desire, is not the category of space. It must be objectified by society, and co-operative action must gradually reveal its properties, i.e., how things can be arranged spatially. Space as a category is not that in which things are perceived, but that in which members of a society co-operate and act together on things. In such social behaviour the private spaces, perceived by individuals, are welded together, and transformed into a public space, an idea transcending all society's several members and imposed upon them. By themselves "above" and "below" are meaningless symbols; in co-operative action they acquire both references and referents, and are given context. In a cave dwelling of the Old Stone Age the children had to learn where they should sleep just as in the collective hunt or ritual dance each adult must occupy his appointed place. In such activities a common spatial world is constructed; the spatial pattern is realized just in moving to take up the socially designated positions and occupying them. Thus men gradually discover by experiment how things and persons can be arranged spatially, so defining an idea of space. As such it must find a symbolic vehicle and be expressed.

The verbal symbol, "space," in English, is a convenient expression like "electricity," but it too is a dangerous one and may mislead. The category may get turned into a "thing" and be hypostatized. We talk of "measuring space," but what we really measure are always fields, or strips of rope or lines on paper, that are spatially extended. The word inevitably suggests some sort of frame into which things have to be fitted. It should mean rather a kind of pattern that men can make if only symbolically. In this correct usage the symbol's meaning has demonstrably changed in the course of history. A radical transformation of Kant's eternal and immutable category is not much over a century old: Euclid's three-dimensional space has grown into the n-dimensional space of Lobochevski and Riemann. More recently Relativity has familiarized most people with the latter idea or at least its symbolic vehicle. If few people understand the concept, most will admit that it has been triumphantly justified by successful operation.

Causality (cause and effect) is a very reputable category, but proves no more immutable and still less *a priori* than space. It was regarded by Kant as the presupposition that made science possible. It has certainly proved a very serviceable scaffolding within which the whole edifice of mechanics and physics since Galileo has been built. But the scaffolding has been bent by the weight of accumulating data it supports and to accommodate unexpected discoveries. And now the distortion has become so acute that it has to be replaced by a fresh scaffolding. Atomic physicists have abandoned causality in favour of mathematical probability. They have been induced to adopt this drastic expedient not by the criticisms levelled against the old category by logicians, but to accommodate fresh empirical data. Their reason suggests that the category of causality is based on experience rather than its prerequisite.

Of course causes of the rather mystical kind excogitated by metaphysicists can be perceived even less than metaphysical space. But action presents every sentient being with a pair of perceptible events that are "causally" connected. By exerting your muscles in pushing against a movable object—an event perceived with the aid of muscular and tactual sensations—the object changes its spatial relation to you and other fixed objects—a second event disclosed by vision. This is the basic perceptual pattern the outline of which, conceptualized and socialized, becomes causality. It might even acquire at the perceptual level the element of "necessity" that was supposedly essential in the category until probability proved a more serviceable idea. This primary pattern, given in private experience, is objectified as soon as it is used as a guide in the distinctively human kind of action represented by the manufacture of tools. The palaeolithic flint knapper not only must have perceived that when he delivered a suitable blow on a flint nodule a flake came off, but he also behaved as if he confidently expected a similar blow on another nodule to be followed by the detachment of a second flake. Now, the act of striking a flint nodule is itself a pattern—a pattern of the kind termed "causal." The operator knows the pattern, if not before or even after, in the act itself. Our operator's confidence was inspired not only by his own memories of successful repetitions of the feat, but still more by the social endorsement of his expectation. For, the reader will recall (page 11), every tool is a social product, and this flint knapper, like every other, had been taught by his society what to make and how to make it. In other words, society had transmitted to him, whether by precept and example or by the latter alone, the idea of the flake to be produced and the idea of how to make it. In his successful act the idea was realized. In other words the correspondence between the ideal reconstruction and the external world was re-established. Therewith the correspondence between the causal pattern as conceived socially and a pattern of the external world was publicly vindicated. Collective experience thus converted the successes of repeated individual experiments into a necessary consequence of socially inculcated actions. The outline pattern discovered and justified in operation becomes a category, a tool for planning further actions.

If generalized into a rule, "Every event has a cause," though long before any such rules were formulated, causality thus conceived inevitably engendered a horde of fictitious beings—gods, spirits, demons . . . to act as causes. It is indeed still replenishing language with their symbols—"gravity" ("the pull of gravity"), "chemical affinity," "the libido" are just attenuated descendants of Jove and Juno! Of course the category has been refined and depersonalized by generations of philosophers and logicians. Even so as Ritchie remarked in the *Natural History of Mind* (1936) "a nasty flavour of pushing and pulling clings to causality." In any case the refinements have been due as much to craftsmen and technicians as to philosophers. In the Old Stone Age the only way men could move things was to push and pull them with their own muscular energy. Neolithic men had domesticated oxen, asses and horses and could make them do some of the pushing and pulling. Scarcely two thousand years ago Greek engineers designed water mills for grinding grain, and therewith men began to control and use for the first time an inanimate motive power. In the last thousand years the Greco-Roman water mill has given birth to varied progeny of complicated machines actuated by inanimate motive powers (water wheels, steam engines, etc.) and applying rotary motion to the performance of an immense variety of repetitive operations formerly executed by hand. Familiarity with machines that European societies could construct and operate completed the transformation of the personal or animistic category of cause into a mechanistic one that since Newton has done such signal service in physics. The outline pattern, imagined on the analogy of machines that men do make but far outstripping human ingenuity to realize, is itself just a vast machine whose motion, being cyclical because all the essential parts just revolve, produces only change in the relative positions of the components, but no really novel configuration. The latest transformation of the "eternal" category in turn is similarly related on the one hand to the invention and construction of electronic machines that are no longer cyclical and on the other to the creation of symbolic vehicles for intellectual tools, e.g., for expressing, and operating with, mathematical probability.

Besides its liability to personification, causality suffers from a further defect. "Events" as perceived are seldom simple, but can be usually analysed into a whole train of events. To the lazy motorist it is a push on the starter button that "causes" the engine to "go." Any mechanic can recognize a battalion of complex processes in delicate mechanisms intervening between the pushed button and the firing cylinders, and a scientist could identify a regiment of subtler reactions behind them! Again even the simplest member of a causal sequence may appear complicated by irrelevant accidents. In trying to make flint implements from a nodule a modern archaeologist often bashes his thumb and adds the utterance of an imprecation to his manual activities. Very likely the Stone Age flint knapper did the same, but perhaps he mistook his expletive for an element in his causal activity as efficient as the movement of his hands. If he transmitted this belief with his practical lore to his apprentices, if, that is, society endorsed his illusion, the imprecation became a magic spell, as essential a "cause" of the finished tool as skill and muscle. Be that as it may, among illiterate societies today effective and rational productive operations, for instance in fishing, in potmaking and in iron smelting, are habitually accompanied or preceded by what we regard as superstitious rites—abstinences, the recital of spells, even bloody sacrifices. These barbarian tribes behave as if they made no distinction between the manual and the ritual action, but regarded both, indissolubly united, as the "cause" of the desired result.

When scientists justifiably boast of their success in discovering causes, they generally mean disentangling an efficient cause from such irrelevant accidents. Still, exponents of every branch of science stop disentangling somewhere— when they have found experimentally the kind of event within the limited field of their particular discipline that "invariably" precedes the particular phenomenon they wish to produce. Causal connexions do correspond to outline patterns of the external world; for in every successful act the causal connexion is realized.

The examples of space and causality should not only have clarified the *rôle* here assigned to the categories, but also have suggested another aspect of knowledge itself. In our simile the architect, in collaboration with the archaeologists, had prepared a provisional design for the reconstructed church, an imaginary picture of the edifice based on the visible surviving traces of its ground plan and incorporating the architectural fragments exposed among the heaps of debris. This imagined picture he communicated to the masons, and in accordance with it they set up a scaffolding, a substantial but skeleton expression of the provisional design. In so far as the skeleton frame was clothed by the builders with stone walls, and window frames and voussoirs rescued from the debris were fitted into their designated places, the architects' design was realized; it had been projected out of the team's head into the external world where they could perceive it with eyes and hands. But the team's success depended not only on the perspicacity of its members in discerning the plan from half-buried wall stumps and the functions that the fragments lying about should fulfil in such a building, but also on their technical ability to set up a skeleton framework to sustain these during the actual re-erection.

The categories are outlines of the patterns, selected from the wealth presented by the external world precisely because they are patterns that men can replicate in action. They have changed in the course of history as men's ability to control the external world has been enlarged with the accumulation of knowledge. It was thus that the mechanistic conception of causality replaced (in certain domains) the personal and animistic ones and is in its turn being transformed before our eyes (page 79). Now an act, deliberate and purposeful, it-self exhibits a pattern. But this pattern is at once "in the head" and "outside it." The ideal pattern (purpose or project) in the actor's head does not just correspond to a pattern of the external world, it is or rather becomes that pattern. The ideal pattern is realized in the action. After the action is successfully completed, the pattern of ideas in the head, representing the result of the action, again corresponds to the resultant pattern in the external world. But in the process of acting there are not two expressions of the pattern corresponding, but the pattern is simultaneously ideal and real.

Actions are of course individual. But much more than even his perceptions (page 56), an individual's actions are deter-mined by his society. From our elders and fellows we learn what we can do and how to do it. Education is not so much pumping socially accumulated information into the young as leading them to behave and teaching them how to act; children are taught to walk and are house-trained. Within varying limits behaviour is controlled by society, and con-formity to approved behaviour patterns is enforced more or less strictly in different societies by law, custom, and public opinion. Finally most effective human action is co-operative, and it is precisely for such action that an ideal reproduction of the external world is needed. Indeed it is in co-operation that the patterns of action whose outlines form bases for categories become objectified (page 76). The categories are modelled on the outlines of patterns of behaviour that are objectified by co-operation in society.

With the aid of categories men are able to imagine the continuation of some aspect of reality's pattern between the moment of knowing and the doing. We have compared them to a scaffolding that enables the builders to anticipate the lines of walls and the location of features in the upper courses to which the replaced material has not yet mounted. Thus the categories are also tools, albeit intellectual tools, used for the ordering of ideas in the head. Like all tools, they are therefore social; individuals do not have to invent or discover the categories for themselves any more than they have to devise the appropriate tool on every occasion. Models for both are normally provided by society. This ensures that the ideal reproductions in the heads of all society's members shall correspond, and in particular it guarantees the correspondence of the anticipation of the future made in imagination by each for co-operative action. If every member of our team of rebuilders set up an independent scaffolding of his own it is unlikely that the Saxon church would ever be rebuilt!

It is owing to their social nature that the categories appear *a priori*, necessary and eternal (page 74). In this sense they are in truth anterior to private experience. They are neither discovered nor invented by individuals, but imposed by society. "An idea is necessary if it imposes itself on the mind by some virtue of its own without proof." This virtue is conferred on the categories by society. For "if men did not agree upon these essential ideas, all contact between their minds and therewith any life together would be impossible."

The life span of a category transcends that of any individual as does society itself, though it is not thereby endowed with immortality. As imposed by society, categories are properly called necessary. A member of any society who planned and acted in accordance with private categories, peculiar to himself, could not co-operate with his fellows and would be treated as insane.

Of course the foregoing account is less than half the story. Human actions all too often fail. Failure means that the ideal pattern did not correspond to that of the external world and was not realized in action. The discordance may be due to defects in the categories used to frame the ideal pattern. The categories have not been revealed to mankind but have been slowly and labouriously discovered, and refined without being perfect even yet.

At this point I ought to introduce a sketch of the development of the categories, based on the data afforded by anthropology, child psychology and written sources. But to spare the reader I shall content myself with a myth—a myth is a story told to account for and justify some social institution or religious rite—to suggest the development of two categories since the Old Stone Age. Imagine a palaeolithic savage: his physical equipment was comparable to that of the Arunta of Central Australia today, and his conceptual outfit may well have been similar. He perceived, outside his head and spatially separate one from the other, clusters of sensations—visual, tactual, olfactory—and learned from experience that similar clusters recurred. But being human, he had learned from his group names for such clusters; sensations crystallized round these symbols which thus came to denote *objects* and these objectified clusters of sensations existed not only for him, but for his whole group. He could perceive, of course, that some sensation clusters were like his own body and others were not. But the names he learned did not emphasize this distinction. Among the Arunta the same name, translated "black cockatoo," is equally applicable to birds, to men, and even to trees and rocks!

All the objects perceived had an immediate or indirect biological relation to our savage; they were perceived as stimuli to instinctive appetites or as obstacles to their satisfaction. But the tribe prescribed social relations to these stimuli that might thwart instinctive reactions; certain appetizing foods were forbidden him, intercourse with some attractive women prohibited. In general his behaviour toward all perceived objects must conform to customary rules that might conflict with innate instincts.

The palaeolithic savage doubtless perceived his sensation clusters as spatially arranged, as forms spatially related to other forms. But he conceived them as organized in accordance with a social pattern that he had very early learned to recognize. Whatever else his elders taught him, they did not neglect to instruct him how to behave toward the several members of his group. For in respect to these he had specific rights and duties which were rigorously defined by custom and enforced by public opinion, backed up, if need be, by physical sanctions. He would have learned, had he been an Australian aborigine, that his society was divided into clans whose mutual relations were prescribed by tradition, while the rights and duties of fellow clansmen one to another were similarly laid down. Now, this social organization embraced *all* the objects perceived in the external world. Among the

Arunta not only men, but animals, birds, insects, plants, hills, rain belong to clans. To them all, therefore, he has the same kind of rights and obligations as to his fellow men. The ideal reproduction of the external world to such savages must then be dominated by this social pattern; the outline of the familiar pattern of social organization provides the overriding category in the reproduction's construction. Even the perceived spatial pattern may itself have been subordinated to and incorporated in this social pattern's outline.

To continue the myth from this point is justification of the category of *thing*. This starts out presumably as the nucleus round which sensations recurrently cluster and which is objectified by its name. The actual sensations would then reveal *qualities,* mysteriously adhering to the object. But this was hardly yet a *thing*. Strictly speaking things should be distinguished from *persons*. Things "have" *qualities,* persons exhibit *characters*. Qualities adhere to things that remain inert, characters are expressed in a person's habitual actions. Persons move themselves, things do not. Persons are members of society, things are excluded. Accordingly one can communicate with persons and persuade them to act by means of verbal entreaties, commands or threats.

Our mythical palaeolithic savage drew no such distinctions. Things and persons alike were members of society, assigned a place in the social organization. The distinction between things and persons is very late in mankind's conceptual development. Even today no languages give it grammatical expression; in two-gender languages, like French and Hebrew, all things are either masculine or feminine; even in three-gender languages like German and Latin relatively few things are neither—i.e., neuter. Even in English a knife *cuts* and flint *flakes*. No wonder then that the palaeolithic flint knapper on page 80 mistook his imprecation for an integral moment in the efficient cause. The mistake was really suggested by language and so prompted by society. The mass of futile and ineffectual practices—the magic rites, religious ceremonies, charms, spells, invocations, sacrifices that we term "superstitious"— follow quite logically from the primeval confusion between things and persons. No, not confusion, but failure to distinguish. Men did not first perceive or conceive inanimate things and then in imagination animate them by infusing into them "souls" or "spirits" fashioned in the image of something they supposed inhabiting their own heads. On the contrary the distinction has only very slowly and laboriously been established, and is not yet universally recognized even in our own societies.

If the failure to make this distinction results in futile behaviour toward things and in a model of reality that will not work, it no less depreciates the notion of personality and encourages an unworthy treatment of persons. "If men have made human elements enter into the idea they have formed of things, they have at the same time made elements from things enter into the idea they have formed of themselves."

At least when depersonalized the category of *thinghood* has proved a very useful scaffolding for our ideal reconstruction of reality. It must then replicate in outline a quite fundamental pattern in the external world. It is certainly very profoundly rooted in traditional habits of human thinking. Most people find it terribly hard to think of anything that is not a "thing"; it is almost harder to express such a thought. But of course both have to be done. A spoken word is real in the sense that it is outside our heads, a physical change in the external world. It passes from you to me and conveys a message. It is not a quality of either. Surely it must be a "thing." The Greeks of Homer's day conceived of words just so—as little winged things that fluttered from my mouth to your ears. The epics repeatedly speak of winged words (ἔπεα πτερόεντα), and even in the fifth century Athenian vase painters depicted little birds flying between Achilles and Hector. Yet a word is not a thing. It lacks that element of durability and permanence traditionally associated with things. The requisite category now has a name—a symbol to express the idea—it is *event,* a word that in this sense has only recently become familiar.

Some element of permanence does seem implied in the category of thinghood if a thing be the nucleus around which the sensible qualities cluster recurrently; for the qualities perceived in sensation obviously change—even if the same object be viewed from two positions. But things can be broken up into bits that are smaller things just as they can be put together to make bigger things. Palaeolithic men could split the nodule into flakes even before he could mount his flakes in a wooden handle to make a composite tool. An Ionian natural philosopher, Democritus, imagined this process of breaking up things into smaller and smaller bits until he reached bits so small that they could not be divided up any more. These bits he christened *atoms.* His idea was revived—on quite independent grounds and in an improved form—by Dalton and so became the fundamental category of nineteenth-century chemistry. Then, however, Rutherford began splitting atoms, and so in atomic physics they have dissolved into still more minute particles—electrons, neutrons, positrons and so on. But these still remain *things* for most operations though for some they are more successfully conceived as events— "probability waves," in fact!

In planning co-operative action the practice of breaking

things up and putting other things together should evoke in our mythical society of the Old Stone Age the rudiments of a higher and more abstract category—*substance*. As things have qualities, substances have attributes perceptible to the senses, but these are not so concentrated spatially and do not include form. The concept was of course modelled on what men made things out of—flint that was broken up into knives and scrapers and spearheads, hairs or sinews that were twisted together into ropes. Things were composed (Latinized form of "put together") of substances which gave them their sensible qualities, but shape and perhaps other qualities were conferred by the maker's formative actions. The category, thus generated out of the manual fabrication of tools, was destined to affect still more profoundly men's operations with ideas and the reproduction of reality thereby built up. Even today it seems as indispensable as thinghood. Hence the questions: "Waves of what?" "Patterns of what?" and hence such answers as "The Aether of Space."

For the manufacture of knives, hammers, ropes, huts, hardness or solidity was perhaps the indispensable attribute of any substance and that is what the adjectival form of the word still means in English. But flames, water, even winds and shadows are things—clusters of sensations; they are therefore made of some substance though this may be ever so attenuated. In the end of course the category dissolved, or rather two main kinds of substance were distinguished at opposite ends of the scale of solidity. The kinds that can be used for building and for tools were called by the Greeks and Romans "wood," the traditional building material of their prehistoric ancestors. We still used the Latin name in the form "matter" (in Spanish its etymological equivalent "madera" still means "wood"). The most attenuated substance was in turn named "breath"—Greek πνεῦμα—more familiar today as the filling of tyres!—Latin *spiritus*. The latter term survives as "spirit."

Though contrasted with matter, spirit was not thereby really dematerialized; it remained a very refined sort of substance deprived of most attributes and in particular invisible and intangible. Into this category fell quite naturally what we call gases together with ghosts, souls and the stuff dreams are made of. Medieval alchemy and pharmacy handled plenty of such spirits; "spirits of salt" (hydrochloric acid) were emitted from salt; "spirits of wine" were exhaled when wine was gently heated in a retort and materialized again as alcohol in the receiver. Beside these materializing spirits it was useless to assert that Spirit is not extended, is not spatial, and it was hardly suggested that it was not "in time"—in a time that was turning into a dimension of space.

In the eighteenth century, gases changed categories and became matter. They were weighed, liquefied and made to drive machines. Matter therewith lost some attributes, but it still had weight or rather "mass," as "weight" was sloughing off its absolute character. Scientists then still clung to substances even more attenuated; heat, light, the Aether of Space, having names, must have a bodily substance to bear these. Now they have lost this body or lost their names. Finally, in 1945, mass itself, the last distinctive attribute of matter, turned into energy! Scientific materialists have become the immaterialists *par excellence*. The grossest materialists today are the self-styled spiritualists with their ectoplasm, their materializations and their spirit world "beyond," but by that very word somewhere in some sort of space, however mysteriously!

One final example. We may suppose that our palaeolithic

savage with the aid of his private senses alone could distinguish between three, four, and five flint chips or dead reindeer or sets of other identical objects. Quite young children and even animals can do that. But that is probably about the limit to which number patterns can be normally grasped at the perceptual level. Small children tend to confuse the number pattern with the spatial pattern of quantity; they consider eight pennies spaced out in an eight-inch row as "more than" the same number of pennies set side by side or in a pile. They cannot perceive "the conservation of number." They can only grasp the one-one correspondence between members of two sets by performing the physical operation of setting them side by side, juxtaposing them one by one. Now, counting is just the same operation when at least one of the sets is made up not of spatially separate things, but of temporally discrete events—in fact, actions. For *number* is a temporal pattern whereas *quantity* or magnitude is spatial.

Palaeolithic hunters in Moravia counted the booty of a hunt by making a notch on an ivory rod for each slain reindeer in the heap round their campfire. There was a one-one correspondence between each act of notching and one reindeer, and the whole resultant series of notches corresponded to the total kill. The series of consecutive acts so to speak *seriated* the heap of slain reindeer and left a record of the kill as a series of identical marks on the *tally*—the rod of ivory.

Thus today's catch could be compared with last month's, provided the latter had been similarly recorded, but only by comparing the two tallies notch by notch, by juxtaposing them physically or "in the head"; for each notch, like the act that produced it, was identical with every other in the set. Society, however, to meet the needs of co-operative action, devised a way of distinguishing conventionally between the several members of such a set. So instead of uttering a series of grunts in counting, a man may articulate "two" as the second event, "three" as the next, and so on. The same result is obtained when the seriated events are not the utterances of articulate sounds, but indications of parts of the body or shifts of beads along a wire in an abacus or counting frame, provided the actions are always performed in the same prescribed order. So in counting on fingers and toes you might always begin with the left little finger, thence proceed to the left thumb, then the right thumb to the right little finger, next the right little toe and so on always ending with the left little toe. But just as the names for the consecutive utterances, like all words, are derived from a social convention and their order is laid down by society, so the order of pointing to fingers and toes is socially prescribed and thus made permanent, and the same is still more obviously true of the beads and wires of the abacus, a material tool the use of which the child learns from its elders. In each case "perceptual number" is converted into "conceptual number" by society, by socially directed actions. It is the use of the socially prescribed symbols (right middle finger in our example is as much a symbol as "eight") that reveals to society's members the *conservation of number*. By the use of the symbol, that is, the child realizes that eight pennies in a pile are still just as much eight as when spread out in a row eight inches long.

This conclusion can be generalized: the patterns, whose outlines become categories, can indeed be perceived as patterns by individuals. But private memory does not suffice to reveal their permanence or conservation. That is discovered co-operatively, incorporated in social tradition and inculcated not so much by verbal precepts as by customarily prescribed re-enactment. The flint knapper's apprentice was not taught that the same cause is always followed by the same effect; he was instructed to repeat the same movement of striking and found that the same result, the detachment of a flake, followed.

Incidentally the discovery by some prehistoric society of "the law of the conservation of number," as just described, was as great an intellectual achievement as the discovery of "the law of the conservation of matter" in the nineteenth century and at least as fruitful. Of course neither is a "law" imposed from above on the external world unalterably. Both are hypotheses that, as guiding rules for human action, have worked admirably. For certain kinds of action—at least of symbolic or ideal action—the "conservation of matter" no longer provides useful rules (e.g., when $M = E$). Perhaps in some branches of higher mathematics "number" too is no longer "conserved." In any case frightful confusions and complications ensued when men first tried to apply the concept of number, based on the series of discrete events "in time," to the measurement of continuous quantities. For example, the discovery of the "incommensurability of the diagonal and sides of a square"—that their lengths could never be divided up into bits or units so small that the side and the diagonal both contained any whole or real number of such units—dealt a staggering blow to the whole fabric of Greek philosophy between 450 and 420 B.C. But for the transformations of this category the reader is referred to any book on the history of mathematics.

If my myth has not given the reader a reliable and documented history of the categories, it should have warned him into what pitfalls their illegitimate use may lead the unwary and has led a venerable company of doctors and divines, logicians and natural philosophers. The reason, too, may perhaps be guessed. The categories were created by society as instruments of co-operative action—to help in the anticipatory reproduction "in heads" of an external world that was to be—but only was to be—the theatre of that action and thereby to guarantee that the reproduction be the same for all co-operators. They were modelled on the sort of things men could do—outline behaviour patterns, in fact. But thanks to the knowledge built up within the framework thus constituted, men's capacities for action have expanded enormously—new tools have been invented, fresh forces of production placed at man's disposal. As a result new categories, new intellectual tools could be devised and were needed. Unfortunately languages took shape when human technology was in the Stone Stage, and language expresses the categories. The normal symbolic vehicles for ideas, words, were agreed upon to represent the things then made and used, the actions appropriate to their spatial manipulation and arrangement and to resultant tangible configurations, and grammar imposes the anthropomorphic categories of that remote period. This limitation imposed on their expression has, as we have seen, gravely hindered the production of fresh ideal tools more suitable to the enlarged field of action they should prepare.

Secondly, a scaffolding may serve quite well to support a bit of wall in actual course of rebuilding up to a certain height; its continuation along the same lines may not frame a complete edifice that is either harmonious to contemplate or faithful to the original design. In fact at any given time society could with the available categories reproduce in imagination a world on which to act with some measure of success. If, however, instead of realizing their ideas in action, men go on imagining along the same lines, they are liable to conjure up "in their heads" a world that is neither harmonious to contemplate (i.e., logically consistent) nor a reliable reproduction of reality to guide action.

The categories have been described by Durkheim as "priceless instruments of human thought which the human groups have labouriously forged through the ages and where they have accumulated the best of their intellectual capital." That is not to say they are immutable. On the contrary an intellectual tool can be replaced by a more efficient one just as much as stone knives have given place to steel ones.

VIII.

Individual and Society

SOCIETY—any society—for our purposes here must be constituted of a plurality of human individuals or *persons* who in fact co-operate and by this co-operation itself become elements in a structure or pattern. But if there can be no society without persons to be its members, so there can be no human individuals, no persons without society. Of course persons are also observable things that can be seen, touched, smelt and heard. As such they are discrete, spatially separate and external one to the other. They have in fact spatial relations and may form elements in spatial patterns. But society is not a mere aggregate of mutually external objects; the pattern of society is not a geometrical pattern of juxtaposed elements arranged in Euclidean space; social structures are not to be formed by putting together discrete constituents like the bricks and rafters of a house. Social relations, the relations between persons, are not external and mechanical but intimate and organic. Members of a society do communicate one with another, act together and feel together.

Of course these human individuals, the constituent members of any society, do differ one from another not only in spatial position but also in perceptible qualities or attributes —in sex, age, stature, hair colour, muscular strength, physique, susceptibility to disease and so on. Most of these peculiarities are biologically innate, transmitted intact from one generation to the next. Innate differences in strength or keenness of vision are easily demonstrable and there is some experimental evidence for equally innate differences in the retentiveness of memory, the capacity for operating with symbols, "intelligence" and so on. These differences in character must have a direct physiological basis—divergences in the functioning or interconnections of neurons or something like that.

But most distinctively human characters are derived directly from society. Most differences in them are due not to nature so much as to nurture—to historical discrepancies in the social life and position of persons after birth. "We speak a language we did not make, employ instruments that we did not invent, invoke rights that we did not found; a treasury of knowledge is transmitted to each generation that it did not gather itself. It is to society that we owe these various benefits" (Durkheim). As we have seen, my knowledge of an orderly external world on which I can act rationally is derived almost entirely from society. The scraps disclosed in sense perception by themselves would make no pattern but fit into the pattern whose outlines society has taught me. Indeed what I perceive with my sense organs is conditioned very largely by my education—by what my elders and fellows have taught me to notice. Society teaches me how to behave with respect to what I thus perceive and does not leave me to rely on innate instincts; it provides rules for conduct, inculcated by example and by precept, often enforced by custom or by law. Each of us does and has done many things because he would "feel odd" or be laughed at or even punished if he did not, and other things in the hope of approbation, applause or even reward,

Many actions, first performed under such social pressure, become habitual and are performed almost as spontaneously and unconsciously as reflex responses without any reference to resultant praise or blame. It is these habitual responses that reveal a person's character, as that term is generally understood. Yet they are the consequences of social pressures and of education in the widest sense of the word. To this extent a human individual's personality is itself shaped by society. So in making, and in order to make, the living thing into a human person, society must and does impose upon it a certain role. This is its—now his, for the thing has now become a person—part as an element in the social structure. But social patterns are not made up of identical units but of persons who are socially different—that is, upon whom society has imposed different roles, so that each fulfills a distinct function in the whole.

This whole is not a sum of units nor even a geometrical pattern of mutually exclusive things. Yet some of the characteristics of such social patterns can be illustrated, albeit very roughly, from geometrical figures which are more familiar. Social patterns should be complementary and simple examples can be drawn as figures. Indeed the term is taken from geometry. The reader first met it in an early lesson in connection with the two angles formed when a straight line meets another; it was then applied to the two adjacent angles which together made up 180 degrees. It is applicable also to two figures that can be joined so as to form a more complex one, as when two right-angled triangles are set base to base to form a square or rectangle. A three-dimensional example would be provided by the threads cut respectively on a bolt and on the nut that fits it. Musicians are familiar with four-dimensional patterns formed by the harmony of two or more themes.

Now, what we perceive in the world of things is not Society, but many societies. Every American or Briton (with perhaps the rare exception of orphans and "stateless persons") is, or has been, whether he like it or no, a member of at least two societies or structured groups of persons. He is, or has been, a member of a family and he must be a citizen of the United Kingdom or the United States. As a member of the first each of us has, or had, assigned him a specific role carrying well-defined reciprocal obligations to parents, brothers and sisters. His rights and duties in respect to father and mother, to elder and younger brother and so on differed. This so-called "natural family" presents the simplest and most universal type of social structure, and owes its character very largely to purely biological factors; the divergence in relations between members is, that is to say, determined primarily by the differences in needs and capacity due to age and sex alone.

But the natural family becomes a human family only as an element in a more comprehensive society just as only so does a living thing become a human individual. If natural families of men could theoretically exist in isolation, they never do so in reality. Neither in ethnography nor in history, any more than in Britain or North America, do we find isolated natural families. All known men are members of a tribe, a nation or a State—of a society, that is, larger and more durable than any natural family within which the latter is incorporated and assigned a place as an *institution*.

The simplest known societies today are composed of enlarged families termed *clans*. The social structure or the pattern of such a society consists of the customarily defined relations between clans, i.e., between clansmen, together with similarly defined relations between functionally distinguished classes of persons. The behaviour of one clansman to fellow clansmen and to members of other clans is prescribed in detail by specific traditional rules. These define whom he may marry, and even with whom he may joke, and lay down a series of reciprocal rights and duties, at once economic, sentimental and ritual, and, as pointed out on page 86, extending to things as well as persons. But even in such simple societies the structure, as in the natural family itself, exhibits an hierarchic aspect. As all children, young and old, male and female owe special duties of obedience, respect and affection to their biological parents, so members of all clans must bow to the authority at least of elders—"the old men" —if not of chiefs.

The structure of a State is enormously more complicated than thát of a tribe, but does not usually define so precisely the roles of its members or subjects. It is of course still hierarchic in that citizens even in a "democracy" owe obedience not only to the abstract authority of laws, but also to the personal authority of a graded order of functionaries, officials, magistrates and ministers, appointed or elected to administer and enforce them.

But the citizen of a State is normally also a member of a church or anti-religious society, of a trade union or a professional association, of a sporting or social club and is likely to be the employee or owner of a business or institution. As such he is a member of one or more *voluntary associations,* to use a technical term. Each of these voluntary associations exhibits some sort of more or less formal structure and so imposes a *rôle* on each of its members. The plain citizen may be a very junior employee in a factory, but at the same time a preacher in the local chapel or the president of his trade-union branch. A man's character is formed and displayed quite as much by the part he plays, or is expected to play, in such voluntary associations as by his role as a citizen. The many-faceted varieties of behaviour, displaying the character of a civilized man, are due very largely to the multiplicity of distinct associations to which he may belong and to the variety of roles he is consequently called upon to play.

In the philosophy of Hegel and in sociological theories inspired thereby such voluntary associations are denied the title "societies." They would be at best "partial societies" that have substance only as subordinate constituents of the State which is the only real society—Society with a capital *S!* Save in totalitarian States, the Hegelian theory is patently false; it is flatly contradicted by empirical data. On the one hand, churches, trade unions and learned societies are often international. In fact the policies of national States and international religious or labour movements have often clashed; for instance, a real conflict of loyalties afflicted papists in England under Elizabeth I and later; even today some scientists feel that the secrecy imposed by the security regulations of their State is hard to reconcile with their duty as scientists to publish their discoveries. In fact, a civilized citizen can thus conceive of a duty to humanity as whole that was beyond the comprehension of a barbarian tribesman; the Latin word *hostis,* meaning at once stranger and foeman, illustrates the inevitable limits of tribal morality. On the other hand, the voluntary associations, just mentioned, are very loosely if at all integrated with the structure of the State. Most are officially ignored; others just tolerated; a few like the Christian church under the Roman Empire or the Communist Party in the U.S.A. are legally banned and vainly persecuted.

Nor does the political State exhaust the social relations between human persons—relations which themselves constitute a pattern and integrate the persons related in a social structure. Firstly, there exist and have existed for many millennia regular economic relations between members of politically distinct societies, be they tribes, nations or States. Some sort of fairly frequent intertribal trade is attested archaeologically at least from the New Stone Age and probably earlier still. Now, in trading, persons enter into reciprocal relations that themselves constitute a structure—an *economic system*. To-day economic systems conspicuously transcend any single political system. Trade relations extend far beyond the frontiers of any existing State. Highly industrialized European States, like Belgium or Great Britain, are dependent for raw materials and even food on imports coming from far beyond their political frontiers. At the same time within most States the economic system is far from coinciding with the political structure. So strikes in public services, whether publicly or privately owned, take the form of putting pressure on the consuming public in order to force the political State to intervene to rectify felt grievances.

Marxists of course contend that the economic pattern ultimately determines the whole structure of a society. The relations between persons as producers or consumers of goods and services should override all other relations. Their contention is undeniably correct to this extent: no society could survive unless its economic structure sufficed to supply its members with the minimum of food and other necessaries demanded for subsistence and reproduction. Therefore a political system that totally prevented the economic system from thus functioning could not last long. But the determining influence of the economic pattern is anything but mechanical. The degree of tolerance is surprisingly high; a political system may obstruct the workings of the economy and cause grave friction for a long time before both break down together or the political order be changed. Wars between States belonging to the same economic system provide the most obvious instance of a head-on clash between economic and political interests. Great Britain and Germany have, however, more or less survived two such wars in thirty years and are busily preparing for a third. An indefinite continuance of such conflicts, like the perpetuation of purely economic conflicts between imperial and colonial nations, must inevitably arrest economic development and threatens the paralysis of science and all distinctively human activities, if not the extinction of the human species. But this inevitable disaster may be postponed for an unforeseeable length of time.

If economic systems be thus international and supernational, it is still more important from our immediate standpoint that the collection and accumulation of information is affected by a society by far transcending the bounds of any national State. Communication is possible even today across political frontiers. Language, its normal instrument, is no more politically than biologically determined. English is the official language in two of the largest contemporary States—the U.S.A. and the United Kingdom together with the dominions of Australia, Canada and New Zealand. Spanish is spoken in a yet larger number of independent States. An American from Massachusetts can converse with an Englishman or an Australian as easily as with a fellow American from Tennessee. All members of a language community can and do communicate as freely as subjects of the same State.

But communication is not restricted to the language community. Messages can be translated (cf. page 44). So ideas can cross linguistic barriers as well as political frontiers. They have been doing so for millennia. What archaeologists call diffusion reflects the transmission of ideas from one distinct society to another. It is probably detectable even in the Old Stone Age and is richly documented in the New.

Nor is communication much more restricted by time than by space. We can and do at least *receive* messages from the past. In so far as we can recover the meanings of their symbols—not only the characters of a script, but all artifacts are to some extent symbols—men long dead are communicating ideas to be fitted into our ideal reproduction of reality. And thus our world of knowledge is itself mainly a structure reared by past generations, preserved and transmitted by a continuing society. The additions made thereto in any year, however revolutionary and exciting they may seem, are a tiny fraction of the organized knowledge that we inherit from past years. In fact Society—the society for which we have made such large claims in previous chapters—must comprise the whole species Homo sapiens—all men alive or dead.

This Society does not exist. The societies that do exist or have existed are very poor approximations thereto. If they be not exactly perversions of the ideal, few are contributing deliberately to its realization. Owing to the frailty of human memory and to actual extermination in war, an incalculable number of inventions and discoveries, potential additions to knowledge, made by preliterate societies have been simply forgotten. During the five thousand years since writing was invented, many documents, indeed whole literatures as in the

Indus valley, have perished. Today the divergences of language, the difficulties of translation, the secrecy imposed by rival commercial interests and by hostile militarist States impede the communication of ideas and the pooling of experience. A precondition for the perfection of knowledge—within the limits laid down on page 67—is the realization of the ideal society. In the meantime each society has its own world of knowledge and is responsible for its own conceptual reconstruction of reality. The conceptual reproduction of the external world in the head of a white Australian scientist differs in almost every respect from that in the head of an Arunta clansman. The two differ not only in content, but also in structure, for they are built in accordance with different categories (page 82). Almost equal discrepancies would divide the world of knowledge of a critical European from that of an Indian Brahman. Who shall decide which "knowledge" is the more true?

IX.

Truth and Truths

IN THE last sentence I admitted that truth is relative; there may be degrees of truth. That admission will shock those who have been accustomed to believe that Truth is an eternal and absolute value. But, however truth be defined, its relativity has been a basic conception implicit throughout the foregoing pages and emerging clearly in the last chapter. So now it is time to come out into the open and prepare to justify the assertion.

In harmony with the terminology here adopted I might define "truth" as the correspondence of the conceptual reproduction of reality with the external reality it should reproduce. It will, however, be more convenient to restrict the term somewhat. Concepts, of which the "reproduction" is made up, exist only as expressed in symbols (page 45)— usually words. But words (including mathematical terms) by themselves and in isolation have no meanings; the meaning is normally determined by their relation to other words or symbols, their position that is in a language pattern. Let us call the language pattern in which symbols have meanings a *proposition*. Then the conceptual model of reality can be called a system of propositions. Truth now becomes a property of propositions. It becomes a correspondence between the meanings conveyed by propositions and the external world. Knowledge would then be a system of propositions which would be true in so far as they correspond with the external world. But knowledge is not a prerogative of my head or yours; only the heads of Society comprehend it, and it is Society that expresses it in a system of propositions.

There can be only one *test* of truth as thus defined, only one criterion by which to decide whether a conceptual reproduction does in fact correspond to the external world. That is action. For we have insisted from the beginning that the function of knowledge is practical; it is to furnish a guide to action. From the propositions that express it, can be deduced practically serviceable rules for behaviour. The success of action, guided by the rules thus deduced, is the decisive test of the truth of the proposition from which they are derived. But of course it is not left to the individual person to make the experimental tests himself. In most cases Society has done the testing for him. The treasury of knowledge transmited to him (page 104) consists for the most part of tested propositions in which he is invited to believe.

It will be convenient to call the propositions in which a society believes "truths" (in contradistinction to truth in the sense of trueness). For the distinction between knowledge as here defined and belief is slender. Beliefs can be held privately by an individual and not shared or endorsed by society whereas knowledge must always be public. What is believed by society is known, and what is known is socially believed. Now, an individual may be said to believe a proposition if he is ready to act in accordance with its prescriptions. The final test of such a belief is of course readiness to die for it. I do not mean only the dramatic testimony of the martyr at the stake or even that of the patient who submits to the surgeon's knife or of the Christian Scientist who refuses the operation. Every day we expose ourselves calmly and indeed unconsciously to mortal risks with perfect confidence in society's implicit assurance that they won't eventuate. I believe that my apartment will not collapse upon me, that the sky will not fall and crush me so firmly that I should be unaware of my belief but that ethnographers tell of peoples who are less confident than the society to which I belong.

It is no doubt unlikely that the obedient patient or the confident householder could formulate as a proposition what he believes. Certainly neither could express the grounds for his belief. Both are incorporated in the system of propositions that express the beliefs and the knowledge of his society. These propositions are the truths known to that society as a whole, but not explicitly to all, or even most, of its members. No one can nor need know all that his society knows.

In the last chapter we saw that Society does not exist, only societies, and each society may, in the manner just indicated, believe a different set of propositions, discordant truths. In the metaphorical language of Chapter VI, each society may erect its own proper and distinctive reproduction of the external world, and the several reproductions or worlds of knowledge may differ in structure as well as in content (page 82) since the categories have been shown to be neither so universal nor so eternal as older philosophies pretended. There thus may be, and indeed are and have been, many divergent and even contrasted conceptual worlds expressed in equally disparate systems of propositions or "truths." That is why there must be degrees of truth. For the several ideal reproductions of reality cannot all correspond equally closely to that reality; they cannot all be equally true in the sense of page 106.

Yet all must be more or less true. Every reproduction of

the external world, constructed and used as a guide to action by an historical society, must in some degree correspond to that reality. Otherwise the society could not have maintained itself; its members, if acting in accordance with totally untrue propositions, would not have succeeded in making even the simplest tools and in securing therewith food and shelter from the external world. None on the other hand can correspond perfectly with the latter for reasons already hinted at previously. Yet some must be truer, i.e., approximate more closely than others to the external world that each claims to reproduce conceptually.

To clarify this somewhat shocking and confusing assertion further, let me apply it to a concrete case, to fragments torn from two historically distinct reproductions of reality, accepted at successive periods by what may be treated as the same society. On our definition the so-called Ptolemaic or geocentric system of astronomy (according to which the Sun, planets and stars, like the Moon, revolve round the Earth) was "true" from say 240 B.C to A.D. 1543. Not only was it universally accepted by Hellenistic society and its cultural heirs in Europe, it did correspond reasonably well with the observable movements of the heavenly bodies. It did in fact enable men to predict eclipses and occultations with reasonable accuracy and thus enabled mariners to find their way about uncharted seas and helped cartographers to map their coasts. In fact it worked, and its successful applications guaranteed its truth (page 59). No doubt it left a few of the phenomena that could be observed without a telescope unaccounted for; no doubt its predictions were not always perfectly accurate and were in any case frightfully laborious to calculate. Yet for the purposes of the Greeks and Romans, of the Arabs and of North Europeans, at least before the Great

Navigations, it worked well enough and accounted for practically everything that could be observed with the technical
equipment then available.

Copernicus' heliocentric system, at least as perfected by
Kepler, accounted just as fully for the observed phenomena,
but far more neatly. As a result the calculation of eclipses and
occultations was enormously simplified, and incidentally the
consequent predictions turned out more accurate. Thus the
Copernican system worked better than the Ptolemaic and
proved more useful to mariners, merchants and generals
crossing the Atlantic to the New World. It was its practical
applications that won social acceptance for the heliocentric
hypothesis. In the sequel advances in applied science, embodied inter alia in the telescope, revealed phenomena
that were absolutely incompatible with the alternative, eventually the parallax of a fixed star from the opposite poles of
the Earth's orbit, the failure to observe which had induced
Hellenistic astronomers to reject the heliocentric system of
Aristarchus. So a new set of true propositions replaced the
old; part of the conceptual reproduction of the external
world was remodelled, but incorporating the old data. Yet,
I repeat, the Ptolemaic system *was* true as long as it enjoyed
unchallenged social endorsement. Beliefs, now dismissed as
errors or mistakes, were once truths.

What has just been said of Ptolemaic astronomy must be
applied with minor modifications to all the publicly held beliefs of the Middle Ages, to the system of propositions expressing the medieval world of ideas. It must apply too to
those of the palaeolithic savage of page 86 and of the Arunta
that were comparable. In the latter cases, of course, the
propositions must have differed in structure as well as in content from any entertained by twentieth-century Europeans—

or for that matter Medieval Europeans or Hellenistic Greeks. Medieval astronomers could have applied the same categories to a geocentric or a heliocentric system. (I have perhaps unduly minimized the far-reaching consequences of shifting the centre of the solar system and replacing circles by ellipses.) The Stone Age in any case had a set of categories indubitably its own. And that was really true of Medieval Europe, Hellenistic Greece, Babylonia in the second millennium B.C., China and other relatively distinct society you might like to mention.

It was comparatively easy to show that the Copernican system was more true than the Ptolemaic. Despite the prolonged resistance of the Roman Catholic Church, that very European society that had inherited, and for generations believed in, the Ptolemaic system as true, was convinced that it was false. If the most potent factor in the reversal of belief was operational, logical arguments, expressed in verbal and mathematical symbols, sealed, if they did not initiate, the inversion. But logical arguments, however ingeniously translated, would not have convinced a Stone Age Arunta nor a Babylonian that the reproduction of the external world, accepted in European society in 1950, is truer than his; for his logic itself was different.

Within our own society, using the symbols, the categories, the treasury of knowledge that society has forged and amassed, we can profitably argue thus: Our world of knowledge is more comprehensive and more coherent and "works" better than any other known to history. Therefore it must be the truest. The Arunta's system brings order to the pooled experiences of a few hundred tribesmen who never wander far beyond their tribal territory of a thousand or so square miles, seldom (before the advent of the whites) hold communication with strangers and keep no written records to preserve accurately the information gathered by past generations. The external world they have to reproduce ideally is tiny. So must have been that of our own palaeolithic forerunners. The Babylonians' world about 1500 B.C. was immensely larger and richer, but still ridiculously small. It systematized the recorded experiences of barely a hundred generations and of merchants, ambassadors, soldiers and slaves whose journeyings were limited roughly by the Nile, the Arabian Sea, the Indus and the deserts of Central Asia. The known world of an American or of an Englishman today comprises most of the contents, though not the form, of the Babylonians' together with those of many other societies as well as our own more immediate ancestors'. For that reason alone it is more comprehensive and should correspond better than any other to the external world that is still immensely larger and richer. We could argue too that our world is the most coherent, most self-consistent and therefore truest.

Neither line of argument would have much effect on a contemporary equivalent of our Stone Age ancestors, say an Arunta, or even of the Babylonians, perhaps a Tibetan. The operational argument might prove more convincing. Our model works better than theirs; our system of propositions yields more reliable rules for a greater variety of actions, and the results can be shown and perceived. Even so it must be remembered that the socially approved ends of action have themselves varied in the course of history and are not the same in every society today—most purposes are as much social in origin as tools are. No Arunta and no Tibetan is consumed with a desire to travel abroad at three hundred miles an hour or to kill thousands of persons he has never seen. Stratocruisers and atom bombs would impress no savage philosopher. On the other hand when material British bullets penetrated the infallible magic armour of Chaka's warriors, they shattered not only black bodies, but also black beliefs. The superior truth of European medicine over magical remedies can be similarly demonstrated by the cure or prevention of diseases. Slowly but inevitably the superiority of our system of propositions both in content and in structure can be demonstrated in practical application. In the absence of any Society embracing all societies, the only test to discriminate between divergent and conflicting systems of truths is operational. By its aid we can unmask as errors what societies have accepted as truths.

But how do such errors arise? How does attempted reproduction of the external world come to diverge so glaringly from the original to which it should correspond? Obviously mere lack of empirical data, the incompleteness of the accumulated information about the external world must in itself cause discrepancies. But the term "error" should perhaps be reserved for positive divergences. It will help toward an understanding of truth if the sources of such error be examined. I would like to distinguish perceptual, conceptual and metaphysical sources of error.

Perceptual errors include both illusions and delusions and affect the sense data, the messages from the external world, on which an ideal reproduction of the latter should be based. Both are familiar subject matter for individual psychology. The stock example of illusion is the straight stick that appears bent when partially immersed in water. You really do *see* the stick as bent, but you can correct the illusion for yourself by appealing to another sense, e.g., touch. Yet even here you have usually learned from society to which sense's testimony you should give credence. Not all illusions could thus be corrected privately by individual percipients. The sun and planets appear to move across the heavens round the earth. You and I actually observe this apparent movement with our eyes and not you and I alone, but all members of every society. The apparent motion is therefore treated as the real motion by all members of society. It is thus objectified and integrated into society's reproduction of reality. The illusion cannot be exposed by an appeal to the testimony of senses other than sight. In fact it required the collation of a vast number of messages received, recorded and published by many co-operating observers widely separated in space and time to expose the illusion. The conclusive exposure indeed required the invention and manufacture of a new tool, the telescope, to supplement the bodily organs of sight. Now every generation learns from society correctly to interpret the message received by the eyes.

Illusions are experiences common to all men and in that sense public. Delusions, however, are private. The individual victim doubtless sees the visions or hears the voices as he claims, but no one else hears or sees them as and when he does. So they cannot be genuine messages from the external world outside his head, but must result from some event or condition inside his skin affecting the visual or auditory nerves. By himself the victim can hardly unveil such errors. The quickest corrective is provided by society; attempts to co-operate with his fellows reveal the discrepancy between his private world and that of society. If this does not banish the delusion, the victim will be regarded as insane.

However, a whole society may accept someone's delusions as truths. His fellows accept his account of what he allegedly saw or heard and act accordingly. A delusion, thus accepted by society, is thereby incorporated in the social reproduction of reality and is objectified. The less a society knows, the smaller the amount of information incorporated in its conceptual reproduction of the external world, and the more gaps there are in the latter, the better chance have private delusions of being believed and included as truths in the system of propositions that express society's world of knowledge. Conversely an individual is liable to imagine he sees or hears what society suggests he might, or even should, see. Among certain Red Indian tribes every youth was expected to see his guardian spirit in a vision. And of course every youth duly saw such a vision though generally only after preparatory fasts and ascetic exercises.

The description, classification and explanation of private errors and mistakes are a matter for individual psychology, not for epistemology. I have mentioned two common kinds, but plenty could be cited. All can be objectified by society. Every kind of mistake, illusion, hallucination, or delusion to which an individual is liable may be taken by his fellows as a genuine message from the common external world or even as an exceptionally precious revelation. What the victim reports is believed by his society and so becomes a truth. The reader will recall of course the close connexion between knowledge—and therefore between belief—and action. Knowledge is to provide rules for action, but rational action is directed to the attainment of some desired end. This intimate nexus is the cause both of many private errors and of their objectification by society as truths. It is this that wins, and for centuries has been winning, credence for the preposterous claims of quacks, magicians, medicine men, soothsayers, shamans . . . and has invested with the glamour of revealed truth the specious or incoherent propositions such assert. Passionate hopes and intense desires common to all members of a society are liable to transform into accepted truths and objectify the most absurd and improbable propositions, provided they promise gratification for these.

It is worth quoting one example. In the first autumn of World War I (1914) when the British public was startled and gravely alarmed by the success of the German armies and the speed of their advance, a quite fantastic tale gained currency in wide and quite well-educated circles in England. The myth related that substantial Russian forces had been landed somewhere in Scotland and had been transported overland by train—by the most unlikely routes at that—across England to re-enforce the hard-pressed British and French troops on the Somme. The story was never printed and I never met anyone who had actually seen "the Russians" himself. But I did meet people—mostly women—who claimed to have the story from an eyewitness. They purported to be repeating what their informants had actually said. They had seen, standing or passing slowly through some station, one or more special trains full of men in foreign uniforms and heavy top boots and—conclusive touch of verisimilitude!—with snow on their coat collars! If such a myth, riddled with improbabilities and absurdities could gain credence among educated Englishmen such as parsons and their wives under the influence of emotional stress in 1914, is it surprising that smaller societies whose knowledge is much narrower, less comprehensive and full of gaps, should believe far more improbable tales, provided these offer hope and encouragement? Of course they not only believe them; they persecute or at least look askance at anyone who dares to express doubt, or to act as if he doubted the socially approved belief.

But let us be fair. They should believe them. To enable

them to sustain long and arduous toil, to endure danger and suffering most men need some assurance of ultimate success, reward, relief. This necessary confidence the spells of the magician and the shaman can and do give, as Malinowski has so ably shown. Though no magic can ensure a good harvest or recovery from disease, it can yet give the cultivator or the patient encouragement to make the efforts which alone can bring the desired result. To that extent in default of knowledge, erroneous beliefs may be socially necessary.

Among conceptual errors the most subtle and persistent are due to a misuse of categories. That has been implicitly dealt with in Chapter VI. It is needless to repeat what was there said save to remind the reader how society sometimes imposes upon its members categories that have become inadequate. In particular the symbolic supports for ideas that society offers us in language, the principal instrument of thinking, may often constitute a stumbling block. All languages took shape in a comparatively early stage of social development. Grammar and syntax are appropriate to a Stone Stage technology when men controlled no motive power save their own muscles, at best supplemented only by that of oxen. Grammatical forms and syntactical usage make little distinction between inanimate and living objects, less between the latter and persons. Actions are confused with qualities and both with things. And all too often the confusing word is sanctified and invested with intense emotional colour.

Conceptual errors can be exposed in precisely the same way as perceptual errors—only in practice, only by human co-operative action. That is really what a distinguished physicist meant when he told the British Association for the Advancement of Science in 1938 "the formal logic which has held the field since the days of Aristotle as the ideal form of reasoning has to be changed *to accommodate the accumulation of empirical data.*" The old conceptual frame of causality just would not work in atomic physics. On the other hand neither perceptual nor conceptual errors, once objectified by society, can be unmasked merely by the exposure of logical contradictions or by repeated failures. It is always possible to hide logical inconsistencies under verbal subtleties and to explain away failures. Error like truth is relative, or rather both are correlative. What once were truths are recognizable as errors only when contrasted with superior truths. Still the latter's superiority can only be vindicated operationally.

X.

My Beliefs

THE foregoing errors are plainly corrigible in theory though not by theory divorced from practice. Hence, if all deficiencies in the conceptual reproduction of reality and all discrepancies between the "two" patterns were due to such errors, perfect knowledge, absolute truth, would be theoretically attainable; a complete correspondence between conceptual reconstruction and real construction would be a possible goal. But the foregoing pages have revealed a source of error inherent in the very structure of reality and therefore incorrigible and absolute. I have insisted repeatedly that the pattern of reality must be at least four-dimensional while the pattern of knowledge, reality as reproduced, is three-dimensional. The reproduction, termed knowledge, based on experience, on messages received from the external world, can only correspond to the structure of that world in so far as the latter is already realized. At any given moment our reproduction is already out of date. We try to bring it up to date by imagining the continuation of the pattern as explained on page 71 and the following. Having recognized a pattern in outline—a category—at the moment of decision, we assume that the same pattern will go on realizing itself till the moment of action, and on that assumption build up our ideal reproduction to guide the action. This much we must assume to be able to act at all, indeed to be able to live.

To hope for perfect knowledge would mean a very substantial enlargement of this assumption. It means in fact assuming that the whole pattern of reality is already here and now complete and perfect and therefore knowable if not yet known. The pattern is therefore "outside" or "above" time and transcends its expression in elements comprehensible in perception. To assume that would be to assert a metaphysical proposition. And so would to deny it. Now, a *metaphysical proposition* is a proposition claiming truth, but by its very nature exempt from any operational test, the sole test of truth here admitted (page 107). Such propositions transcend the bounds of experience and therefore can form no part of the system that we have termed knowledge. They express *beliefs* only. The stock questions that philosophy is expected to answer—What is Reality? Truth? the Good? Beauty? the Meaning of Life?—can only be answered by metaphysical propositions. In so far as I have suggested answers, I have committed myself to such beliefs. But most metaphysical systems imply transcendence. This I have denied—admittedly in a metaphysical proposition.

Philosophical systems are generally classified as either materialist or idealist. The basis of classification is of course the answer given to the question: What is Reality made of? I hope after Chapter VIII that the reader will realize that the question is just silly. It will make no sort of difference whether you answer "Matter" or "Spirit"—at least as long as you conceive "spirit" as a kind of stuff out of which things can be made. The really significant question is "How is Reality constructed?" or rather "How does it function?" To that, too, materialists and idealists have different answers, though they are seldom clearly formulated. Each school starts with a model, already known and given in experience and imagines it enlarged, refined and glorified, till its behaviour patterns might replicate the infinitely varied behaviour of the whole known world.

The materialists' model is the machine, the sort of machine with which Europeans became familiar and which they employed with such startling success after 1700—I mean water mills and steam engines employing rotary motion. Their actions grew ever more complex. As you watched the wheels revolve slowly you experienced a series of new sensations. But only for a time; after one complete revolution the same sights were presented to your eyes in the same order. The series was repetitive—a cycle. Significantly enough similar cycles of visible phenomena had long been familiar on a far grander scale in the movement of the heavenly bodies. In imaginations thus inspired the machine could be magnified indefinitely and enriched with ever more complicated accessory mechanisms. But its behaviour still remained repetitive; the essential pattern was adequately recapitulated in the revolving driving wheel. However many sympathetically rotating gadgets, like the epicycles of Ptolemaic astronomy, were introduced, nothing really new ever eventuated, the same events recurred again and again. And they were all there before the machine was made. A machine can do that and only that which it is constructed to do. All its actions are predetermined by the design, specified to the minutest detail in the blueprint followed by its builders. The design thus transcends the machine.

A time sequence might be marked and measured by stages in the driving wheel's revolution in relation to the stationary frame. But the design existed before the revolution began and will exist after its completion in a distinct external frame of reference—from the machine's standpoint, changeless and eternal. On the other hand within an entirely self-contained machine with no fixed parts—if a machine without a frame could be imagined—there would be no time to measure since every point on a circle and every moment in its revolution is indistinguishable from any other. But any real machine has a frame, it has a maker and began to function. So however hard you try to imagine the universe as an enormously vast and immensely complicated machine, you inevitably get back to something transcending it and supporting it—in a word to God. So materialism in this form breaks down as a metaphysical account of the Universe. Mechanism as a model for reality has in fact been abandoned—but not only for the reasons just given. Thanks to fresh technical inventions and scientific knowledge men can now construct machines that are not cyclical. Their actions are apparently not precisely predetermined by the design nor exactly built in by the makers.

The idealists' model is Mind—the human mind as disclosed privately in introspection but imagined as functioning autonomously without any sensuous content derived from outside through perception. The German Hegel, whose system is the most stupendous and the most consistent exposition of idealism, claims to show how the bare categories, pure ideas without sensible content or symbolic support, must develop through the logical dialectic inherent in their nature, and to deduce therefrom the whole of natural and human history as the self-revelation of the Absolute Idea or Reason. The latter, of course, is just another name for God and transcends the whole process of which it is at once the beginning and the predetermined end. Here, too, there is no room for real innovation, no creation of new values.

Indeed Hegel's "God" or "Absolute" is suspiciously like Hegel himself—an imaginary and highly idealized Hegel. There is indeed no doubt that Hegel's *Staat* is just the Prussian State—not indeed the Prussian State of Hegel's day, but what he and other liberals hoped the Prussian State would soon become. Yet he deduces this *Staat* and presents it as the necessary and fore-ordained outcome of a dialectical process, the only possible organization of society in which alone the conflicting claims of all persons could be reconciled and personality achieve perfection. Just so one feels that Hegel looked into his own head—a head well stocked with ideas derived from the external world and especially from his philosophical predecessors—and described the reasoning processes he thought he could observe there as Reasoning itself, the necessary and exclusive pattern of all rational thinking, the thought of God Himself.

Transcendence cannot be proved or disproved by the decisive test of practice; it should transcend experience. In denying it I assert a metaphysical proposition. Henceforth I shall state what I believe, not what I claim to know, and shall enunciate beliefs that may not be truths. I believe then that the pattern of Reality—I do know that it is patterned—is at least four-dimensional. Reality is an activity, a process that is neither repeating itself over and over again nor yet is approximating to a predetermined goal or the realization of a preconceived plan. It is on the contrary genuinely creative, constantly bringing forth what has never been produced before, genuine novelties.

I could indeed adduce arguments in support of this thesis. Half a million years of human history show not only some repetitions, but much more the repeated emergence of novel inventions, unprecedented patterns of behaviour and of social organization, fresh needs, desires and aspirations, in a word new values. In natural history "natural selection" is "a mechanism for generating an exceedingly high degree of improbability." Again the replacement of the category of mechanistic causality by that of probability in atomic physics (page 77) is equivalent to a rejection of transcendence by the very natural scientists whom Hugh Millar in 1939 described as the last bulwarks of transcendentalism. I do not deceive myself into believing nor do I ask the reader to believe that the foregoing "arguments" were the grounds for my belief nor proofs of its validity. I shall just assume in the sequel that the pattern of Reality does not transcend its expression in history, that in fact there *is* no complete pattern of, or plan for, Reality, past and future, laid up somewhere or somehow as the blueprint for a miraculous machine or a bodiless idea in the mind of God.

That is not to deny any pattern, any order to Reality, or to suggest that the pattern that will unfold is arbitrary, capricious and unrelated to the knowable realized pattern expressed in History. On the contrary it must be a continuation and development of the existing pattern, already realized and knowable, and therefore determined by the latter in general but not in detail. Creation is not making something out of nothing, but refashioning what already is. Any creative process, whether the painting of a picture, the composition of a symphony or the elaboration of a logical argument, illustrates precisely this combination of continuity and determinacy with flexibility and freedom.

In writing this book and each section of it I knew in advance the sort of thing I planned to say and more or less the conclusion to be reached. Yet I admit that, as I wrote, I saw new arguments and changed my line of approach more than once. None of these innovations nor changes were arbitrary; they did not come to me as inspirations out of the blue. They appeared to me—and I hope the reader will find them so—logical consequences of ideas I had just expressed and written down. They have, I confess, entailed some revision and rewriting of chapters already completed, but not so as to change the general sense. To me, at least, what was expressed determined and made inevitable the next step. Yet I had not anticipated the latter. The pattern of ideas, expressed on page 33, for example, was not and never had been consciously in my head when I wrote the previous page; I hope it has not been in anyone else's head and is therefore "original." I do not remember having seen quite that argument in any book.

The reader may complain that he does not understand and can see no logical necessity in my arguments, and remains sceptical about "creation" that is at once "free" and "determined." I can only ask such to try an experiment. Here I have started a "limerick":

> There once was a peer named deVere
> Who said to his lady, "My dear,
> At a very low price

Now complete it. You are free to do so as you will, subject only to certain limitations determined by the metrical pattern imposed by convention on all limericks, by the grammatical structure of the English language, and by the logical consistency that even nonsense verses should display. Prosody demands that the next line shall contain five or six syllables, three accented, and end in "-ice," the last line four accented syllables and terminate in "-eer." Grammar requires a principal verb with a noun or pronoun as a subject fairly soon. Finally to make sense the principal verb must be something like "buy" or "sell." The metrical pattern is fully known in advance; so in effect is the grammatical structure. The logical consequences are still wide open though "price" points to one or other of two kinds of behaviour (buying or selling) and "low" accords better with the former. But after all this is a "nonsense rhyme" and the anticipated behaviour need not be what our society would call "rational" though it must still bear some contextual relation to "price"; "Cows can walk on ice" just would not make enough sense even for nonsense!

I am not the least perturbed if my description of Reality as a creative activity of process makes perfect knowledge and absolute truth unattainable. The function of knowledge is practical, to guide action. The success of the human species, the sole known society of knowers, in half a million years suffices to demonstrate that sufficient knowledge is attainable. In fact society can not only perceive bits of Reality, but can also apprehend outlines of Reality's pattern, and using them as categories can often anticipate successfully the further development of that pattern. The metaphysical error due to the inevitable discrepancy between Reality as known and reproduced "in heads" and Reality a moment later as the object of action is not fatal. Society can know enough to act and not only act successfully but actually to progress.

For me that is enough. I am not interested in absolute truths, objects of pure contemplation in a supra-sensuous world of ideas, existing eternal, exempt from change or disturbance by human action, set like stars in a remote firmament beyond the reach of society. Such an absolute truth is, I maintain, just as much a fiction as any centaur. Pure contemplation is no more creative activity than is the cyclical movement of a wheel. Knowledge is not to be contemplated but to guide action. That is not to say that the pursuit of knowledge for its own sake, pure science, is futile or meaningless. Major scientific discoveries of the greatest practical utility were indubitably made for precisely that motive without any reference to possible use. Yet the practical results, however long delayed, provide the sole conclusive test of the truth of the discovery, the proof that it is a contribution to knowledge and not just a new superstition. The Babylonian diviners observed and recorded peculiarities of the entrails of sacrificial victims just as accurately and scrupulously as geneticists examine and note down the shape, colour and wrinkles of peas. If we say that the latter have added to knowledge while the soothsayers did not, we mean that the geneticists taught men to grow better peas while the soothsayers' comparable labours bore no comparable fruit.

I am an archaeologist and devote my time to trying to gather information about the behaviour of men long since dead. I like doing this and my society pays me quite well for doing it. Yet neither I nor society can see any immediate practical applications for the information I gather; we are indeed quite sure that it will not increase the production of bombs or butter. Still, we like to think that even archaeological knowledge may someday prove useful to some society. Indeed I might even venture to hope that the archaeological knowledge embodied in the present book may be useful in helping its readers to think more clearly and so to behave more humanly.

Both as an archaeologist and an amateur philosopher I

am interested only in the knowable. The unknowable is as irrelevant to the active quest for knowledge, the collection, classification and interpretation of messages received through sense perception as to more practical kinds of action. Knowledge must still be a guide to action, if only to the acquisition of fresh knowledge.

I confess that in the foregoing pages I have adopted a standpoint, technically and disparagingly termed "naïve realism." Have I not assumed an "external world" "outside" my head but perceptible by sense organs, and contrasted it with an "ideal" or "conceptual world" "inside my head"? Have I not even assumed that "the external world" exists waiting to be perceived and known, independently of anyone perceiving and knowing it? Have I not thereby reasserted the fundamental dualism of "matter" and "spirit"? Have I not indeed added a third term in speaking of Society? For in so doing I seem to postulate not only my own head, but heads waiting to be perceived and known, but at the same time perceiving and knowing.

Not quite. In disclaiming all interest in absolute truths, I have renounced any title to talk about things just "waiting to be perceived and known," what Kant called "things in themselves." I can say nothing about such. Knowledge as I have defined it must be communicable and therefore expressible in symbolic patterns—in propositions. Ineffable truths are not truths at all. But the only vehicles for the expression of truths are the conventional symbols of language—a language which took form in the Stone Age. Its words are therefore sometimes inadequate to the concepts of the twentieth century. The spatial terms "outside," "inside" and "external" have been used in a rather metaphorical, and, to that extent, misleading sense. Obviously if ideas or concepts be—in a sense—"inside heads," they are in no sense confined therein. Similarly if Reality be largely "outside" my head, and even "outside" the hydra heads of Society and to that extent "external," ideas are still, as I have insisted, real and incorporated in Reality. Knowledge too is real and part of Reality. The ideal or conceptual reproduction of Reality not only corresponds to Reality, but is a part or an aspect of, or moment in, Reality. Its pattern not only corresponds to, but by that very fact coincides with, the pattern—or at least a pattern—of Reality. If Reality is a creative process, its conceptual reproduction as knowledge is not a new process but a component of the process itself. In acting, men do not act on Reality, but participate in the activity that is Reality. You may call Reality "spirit" if you mean thereby creative activity, not if you mean a stuff, however refined. You may just as well call it matter, but only in the sense that in atomic fission, $M = E$. I should rather call it Society, but that might be too reminiscent of aboriginal Australian categories.

So far I have been keeping within the bounds of possible experience and trying to describe in admittedly inadequate and often ambiguous symbols what might be empirically given. In conclusion let me merely state some beliefs that could not be thus validated nor verified by any operational test. The creative process that I call Reality is completely self-contained and self-sufficient. Outside it there can be nothing. Therefore it is not made of anything, whether matter or spirit, or by anyone, call it God or Absolute. Apart from the process there are no individuals, no persons. Yet to the process, each individual, though a part, can yet contribute and thus can actively participate in creation itself. For we have seen that there can be no person outside society and no society not composed of persons. At the same time

Society is immortal, but its members are born and die. Hence any idea accepted by Society and objectified is likewise immortal. In creating ideas that are thus accepted, any mortal member of Society attains immortality—yes, though his name be forgotten as completely as his bodily form dissolve. Personally I desire no more. I cannot conceive of a person or Self bereft of its material mortal body any more than I can conceive of an idea detached from any sensible symbolic vehicle.

In denying transcendence, I frankly reject at the same time the possibility of apprehending Reality by any means save the cognitive processes described in this book. There is no short cut to knowledge. Just because Reality is a creative activity, knowledge, to correspond to it, must in turn be a creative activity. Hence I must deny the revelation in religious experience, whatever that may be, of any Reality transcending the process. That is not to deny all value to such experience, but only cognitive value—truth. At its lowest, religion, like the magic described on page 117, may give men the assurance necessary to enable them to maintain the strenuous activity of participation in the creative process that is Reality itself. At its highest it is as members of an imaginary Society, the Kingdom of God, that human beings may become the creators of new values and originate new ideals of the Good and of Beauty. But I still deny any absolute or eternal value to the ideals thus imagined, because they are imagined. Imagination, like any other kind of creation, is not making something out of nothing, but reshaping and recombining in a new way what is already known. Imagination is thus conditioned by experience and can only just advance the boundaries of knowledge a small step.

Society is the repository of all values, the ultimate arbiter of Truth, Goodness and Beauty. These are not eternal values, stored up in remote tranquillity. They have demonstrably varied in the course of human history and will no doubt continue to change. For Society is an unrealized ideal. The Good, the True or the Beautiful is just what Society establishes as the standard. We know in history only societies, and therefore different standards of Goodness, Truth and Beauty, and these may conflict. We can of course imagine a single Society embracing all men—such an ideal has in fact been entertained in Europe since the Stoics in the days of Alexander the Great. Towards such an imaginary Society, men conceive themselves bound by obligations overriding those due to any separatist State or church.

Such flights of imagination may be just masks for cowardice and laziness. Yet it is through them that fresh moral values have in fact emerged in the course of history, and such transvaluation of values is the most obviously creative aspect of the process of Reality. On the other hand in history the moral reformer has only improved upon and refined the moral standards of his own society. The Moral Law of Kant is just a refined formulation of the approved practice of early nineteenth-century pietism while Hegel similarly dignified the standards of behaviour that would have been encouraged by a liberalized Prussian State.

Already it is possible to see why the Humanist ideal is not absolute or final. It is possible to imagine a society comprising more than humanity. Indeed scientists have hinted that humanity may owe a duty to non-human nature, and that not only in the generally recognized utilitarian sense of conserving natural resources for more economical human exploitation.